BETTY CROCKER'S
Easy
Oven Meals

Photography Director: Len Weiss

Illustrator: Bill Goldsmith

Golden Press/New York

Western Publishing Company, Inc.

Racine, Wisconsin

First Printing, 1973

Copyright © 1973 by General Mills, Inc., Minneapolis, Minn. All rights reserved.

Produced in the U.S.A.

Library of Congress Catalog Card Number: 73-78389

TO BEGIN WITH...

The next-best thing to a home-cooked meal that fixes itself is the meal that *tends* itself. An oven meal is just that. Once you shut the oven door, there's little or no watching involved. You're free to turn your back and do whatever else needs doing.

The idea behind *Easy Oven Meals* is to help you get the most out of your oven, engaging it for double and triple duty. All the menus feature at least two foods baked at the same temperature, although not always for the same length of time. (A kitchen timer in good working order will be one of your handiest accessories.)

As you thumb through the pages of this book, you'll see how ingeniously your oven can turn out an almost endless combination of main dishes, side dishes, breads and desserts. The oven recipes are given throughout, along with suggestions and hints for completing the meal. And to help you schedule the put-ins and take-outs, there's a convenient timetable at the beginning of each menu.

The Right Equipment

The proper utensils are important but should be no problem. Such a tremendous variety of sizes, shapes and materials is available that you can choose practical and attractive oven-to-table furnishings without spending a great deal of money. If you are buying new, stick to the standard sizes for which most recipes are written. Look into some of the easy-to-care-for finishes, and shop for pieces that are as at home on the table as they are in the oven. Different types of ovenware have different purposes and advantages. Take a look at the chart on the following page and decide which will be most useful to you (you'll want to have a variety). Remember always to follow any special instructions the manufacturer may include with the utensil.

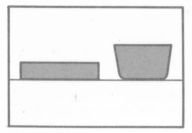

A. One-rack oven arrangement

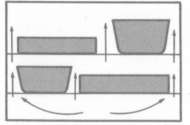

B. Two-rack oven arrangement

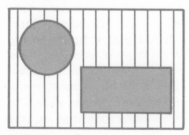

C. Top rack

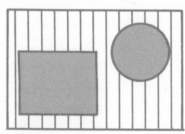

D. Bottom rack

Type of Ovenware	Advantages	What to Look For
Oven-to-table baking dishes (ovenproof glass, enameled metal, stoneware, etc.)	Versatile. Cut down on dish-washing. Wide choice of patterns and styles.	Covered dishes the most useful. Should withstand broiler heat for top-browning.
Ovenproof skillets, Dutch ovens	Multipurpose; go from range top to oven.	Tight-fitting lids, ovenproof handles and knobs.
Freezer-to-burner-to-oven-to-table pieces	Most versatile. Virtually indestructible.	Lids that fit snugly (or you can use aluminum foil).
Open roasting pan with rack (oven-proof glass, metal)	A must for roast-ing meats and poultry evenly.	Heavy, seamless construction, easy-to-grasp handles.
Disposables (alu-minum foil pans, roaster bags, etc.)	For when conve-nience matters—no cleanup.	Sturdy products, the right size for the recipe.

Oven Cookery Tips

☐ Baking times are based on preheated ovens; preheat yours!

☐ When using one oven rack, center the food. Distance from top of food to top of oven should measure about the same as that from pan bottom to oven bottom. Allow space at top for foods that rise. (See diagram A.)

☐ When using both oven racks, try to divide oven in even thirds. For good heat circulation, stagger pans so one is not directly over another. (See diagrams B, C, D.)

☐ Pans should never touch each other or side of oven. A 1½- to 2-inch clearance all around will permit air to circulate and foods to bake evenly.

☐ Ovens vary a bit, so check for doneness at the minimum time given, especially the first time you try a recipe.

TIME-TAMER

Beef and Sausage Stew
Romaine-Radish Salad
Cheese Biscuit Squares
Peach Crisp

OVEN SCHEDULE

35 minutes before serving:
Bake stew (place on lower rack of oven).
20 minutes before serving:
Bake dessert (place on lower rack of oven).
15 minutes before serving:
Bake bread (place on upper rack of oven).
If using a larger oven (30-inch), all foods can be baked on one rack.

BEEF AND SAUSAGE STEW

2 tablespoons salad oil
1 package (5 ounces) little smokie sausage links*
1 pound ground beef
1 package (5 ounces) rotelle (spiral) macaroni or 1½ cups uncooked elbow macaroni
2 cans (16 ounces each) stewed tomatoes
1 can (8 ounces) tomato sauce
1 can (6 ounces) tomato paste
2 tablespoons instant minced onion
1 tablespoon garlic salt
1 teaspoon basil leaves
1 teaspoon oregano
½ teaspoon pepper
2½ cups boiling water

Heat oven to 400°. Heat oil in Dutch oven; brown sausage links over medium heat. Add ground beef; cook and stir until brown. Drain off fat. Stir in remaining ingredients. Cover and bake until macaroni is tender, about 35 minutes.

6 servings.

*You can substitute ½ package (12-ounce size) Polish sausages, Galician sausages or smoked thuringer links, each cut into 3 or 4 pieces, or 1 package (5½ ounces) little wieners for the little smokie sausage links.

CHEESE BISCUIT SQUARES

2 cups buttermilk baking mix
½ cup water
2 tablespoons soft butter or margarine
2 tablespoons grated Parmesan or shredded Cheddar or mozzarella cheese

Heat oven to 400°. Mix baking mix and water to form a soft dough. Turn onto greased baking sheet; spread or pat into rectangle, 10×8 inches. Spread butter on rectangle and sprinkle with cheese. Bake until golden brown, 12 to 15 minutes. Cut into squares.

6 servings.

PEACH CRISP

1 can (21 ounces) peach pie filling
1½ cups buttermilk baking mix
⅓ cup brown sugar (packed)
½ teaspoon cinnamon
¼ teaspoon nutmeg
1 egg
¼ cup shortening, melted

Heat oven to 400°. Spread pie filling in ungreased baking pan, 8×8×2 inches. Stir baking mix, brown sugar, cinnamon and nutmeg in bowl. Beat egg thoroughly; pour onto mixture in bowl and stir until crumbly. Sprinkle evenly over pie filling; drizzle with shortening. Bake until topping is golden brown, about 20 minutes. Serve warm, with ice cream or light cream if desired.

6 servings.

FARMLAND FARE

Individual Barbecued Meat
Loaves
Hash Brown Casserole
Mixed Vegetable Medley
Lettuce Wedges
with Favorite Dressing
Apple Crunch

Pictured on page 23

OVEN SCHEDULE

50 minutes before serving:
Bake meat loaves, potato casserole (place on lower rack of oven), vegetables and dessert (place on upper rack of oven). If using a larger oven (30-inch), all foods can be baked on one rack.

INDIVIDUAL BARBECUED MEAT LOAVES

1 egg
⅔ cup milk
½ cup quick-cooking oats
2 teaspoons salt
¼ teaspoon savory leaves
⅛ teaspoon pepper
1 tablespoon snipped parsley
1½ pounds ground beef
½ cup coarsely chopped onion
Barbecue Glaze (below)

Beat egg slightly in large bowl; mix in remaining ingredients except glaze. Shape mixture into 6 individual loaves and place in ungreased baking pan, 11¾×7½×1½ or 9×9×2 inches. Bake uncovered in 350° oven until done, about 45 minutes, brushing loaves with Barbecue Glaze 3 or 4 times during baking period.

6 servings.

BARBECUE GLAZE

Mix ⅓ cup catsup, 1 tablespoon brown sugar and 1 tablespoon prepared mustard.

About ⅓ cup.

HASH BROWN CASSEROLE

1 can (10½ ounces) condensed cream of celery or cream of mushroom soup
1¾ cups milk
3 tablespoons chopped onion
2 tablespoons chopped green pepper
½ teaspoon salt
⅛ teaspoon pepper
1 package (5.5 ounces) hash brown potatoes with onions

Heat oven to 350°. Mix all ingredients except potatoes; stir in potatoes. Pour into ungreased baking dish, 8×8×2 inches, or 2-quart casserole. Bake uncovered until potatoes are tender and golden brown, 45 to 50 minutes.

6 servings.

MIXED VEGETABLE MEDLEY

1 package (9 ounces) frozen green beans
1 can (16 ounces) whole tomatoes, drained
2 stalks celery, cut into ¼-inch diagonal slices (about 1 cup)
2 medium carrots, cut into ¼-inch diagonal slices (about 1 cup)
½ green pepper, cut into strips
1 teaspoon salt
2 tablespoons butter or margarine

Heat oven to 350°. Rinse green beans with small amount of running cold water to separate and remove ice crystals; drain. Mix all ingredients except butter in ungreased 1½- or 2-quart casserole. Dot with butter. Cover and bake until carrots are crisp-tender, about 45 minutes.

6 servings.

APPLE CRUNCH

1 can (21 ounces) apple pie filling
⅓ cup brown sugar (packed)
¾ cup all-purpose flour*
⅛ teaspoon cinnamon
⅓ cup butter or margarine

Heat oven to 350°. Pour pie filling into ungreased baking pan, 8×8×2 inches, or 9-inch pie pan. Mix remaining ingredients with fork until crumbly. Sprinkle on pie filling. Bake until topping is light brown, 40 to 45 minutes. Serve warm, with cream, ice cream or hard sauce if you wish.

6 servings.

*Do not use self-rising flour in this recipe.

PASTA PERFECT

Shortcut Lasagna
Romaine-Zucchini Toss
Garlic Toast
Cherry Ice Cream
Almond Brownies

OVEN SCHEDULE

55 minutes before serving:
Bake lasagna (place on lower rack of oven) and brownies (place on upper rack of oven).
20 minutes before serving:
Bake toast (place on upper rack of oven).
If using a larger oven (30-inch), all foods can be baked on one rack.

SHORTCUT LASAGNA

1 **pound ground beef**
1 **medium onion, chopped (about ½ cup)**
½ **teaspoon salt**
⅛ **teaspoon garlic powder**
1 **jar (15½ ounces) spaghetti sauce**
1 **carton (12 ounces) creamed cottage cheese (1½ cups)**
¼ **cup grated Parmesan cheese**
2 **teaspoons parsley flakes**
4 **ounces lasagna noodles, cooked and well drained**
3 **packages (4 ounces each) shredded mozzarella cheese (1½ cups)**

In medium saucepan, cook and stir meat, onion, salt and garlic powder until meat is brown and onion is tender. Stir in spaghetti sauce; simmer 15 minutes, stirring occasionally.

Heat oven to 350°. Mix cottage cheese, Parmesan cheese and parsley flakes. In ungreased baking dish, 11¾×7½×1½ inches, layer half each noodles, sauce, mozzarella cheese and cottage cheese mixture; repeat. Cover and bake 40 to 45 minutes. Let stand at room temperature 10 minutes. Cut into squares.

6 servings.

GARLIC TOAST

½ loaf (1-pound size) French bread
¼ cup soft butter or margarine
2 tablespoons snipped parsley
¼ teaspoon garlic powder

Heat oven to 350°. Cut bread diagonally into 1-inch slices. Mix remaining ingredients; spread on cut sides of slices. Place on ungreased baking sheet. Bake until crisp and golden brown, about 20 minutes.

About 12 slices.

ALMOND BROWNIES

2 ounces unsweetened chocolate
⅓ cup shortening
1 cup sugar
2 eggs
½ teaspoon almond extract
¾ cup all-purpose flour*
½ teaspoon baking powder
½ teaspoon salt
½ cup chopped nuts

Heat oven to 350°. Grease baking pan, 8×8×2 inches. In medium saucepan, melt chocolate and shortening over low heat, stirring constantly. Remove from heat. Mix in sugar, eggs and almond extract. Stir in remaining ingredients. Spread in pan. Bake until brownies start to pull away from sides of pan, 30 to 35 minutes. Cool slightly. Cut into 2-inch squares.

16 brownies.

*If using self-rising flour, omit baking powder and salt.

NOTE: To save time, prepare 1 package (15.5 ounces) fudge brownie mix as directed except—stir in ½ teaspoon almond extract.

Take a shortcut to sunny Italy via a speedy new lasagna that's as flavorful as the old favorite. Your time-savers: spaghetti sauce in a jar and cheese already shredded. Handy head starts these are, too, for this inspired family dinner or late-night company supper.

The Garlic Toast is an "of course" accompaniment, and so is the quick-fix salad with an Italian accent. Just combine bite-size pieces of romaine and iceberg lettuce (romaine alone will do nicely, too). The zucchini needn't be pared—just thinly sliced. And while you're about it, slice up some crisp radishes and a couple of green onions for color and zing. Toss lightly with bottled Italian dressing just before serving.

FIT FOR A CZAR

Hamburger Romanoff
Orange-glazed Beets
Tossed Green Salad
Rhubarb-Strawberry Shortcake

OVEN SCHEDULE

55 minutes before serving:
Bake hamburger casserole (place on lower rack of oven).
35 minutes before serving:
Bake beets (place on lower rack of oven) and shortcake (place on upper rack of oven).
5 minutes before serving:
Sprinkle cheese on hamburger casserole.
If using a larger oven (30-inch), all foods can be baked on one rack.

HAMBURGER ROMANOFF

1 **pound ground beef**
1 **can (6 ounces) sliced mushrooms**
1 **envelope (2½ ounces) sour cream sauce mix**
2 **tablespoons flour**
2 **tablespoons instant minced onion**
2 **tablespoons catsup**
1 **teaspoon salt**
½ **teaspoon garlic salt**
¼ **teaspoon pepper**
5 **ounces uncooked noodles (about 3 cups)**
3½ **cups boiling water**
½ **cup grated Parmesan cheese**

Heat oven to 350°. In large skillet, cook and stir meat over medium heat until brown. Drain off fat. Stir in mushrooms (with liquid), sour cream sauce mix, flour, onion, catsup, salt, garlic salt and pepper. In ungreased 2½-quart casserole, layer half each of the uncooked noodles and the meat mixture; repeat. Pour boiling water on top. Cover and bake 50 minutes. Sprinkle with cheese and bake uncovered until golden brown, about 5 minutes.

4 servings.

ORANGE-GLAZED BEETS

1 can (16 ounces) small whole beets, drained
3 tablespoons orange marmalade
1 tablespoon vinegar

Heat oven to 350°. Place beets in ungreased 1-quart casserole. Mix marmalade and vinegar and drizzle on beets. Cover and bake until beets are hot, about 30 minutes.

4 servings.

RHUBARB-STRAWBERRY SHORTCAKE

1½ cups buttermilk baking mix
½ cup sugar
1 egg
½ cup water or milk
2 tablespoons shortening
1 teaspoon vanilla
1 package (16 ounces) frozen rhubarb, thawed
¼ cup strawberry preserves

Heat oven to 350°. Grease and flour baking pan, 8×8×2 inches. In small mixer bowl, blend all ingredients except rhubarb and preserves on low speed ½ minute, scraping bowl frequently. Beat on medium speed 4 minutes, scraping bowl occasionally. Pour into pan. Bake until wooden pick inserted in center comes out clean, 30 to 35 minutes. Cool slightly.

Cut 4 servings from cake; split each serving horizontally. Mix rhubarb and preserves; spoon rhubarb mixture between layers and on top. Serve warm. If desired, top with sweetened whipped cream or Sour Cream Topping: Mix ½ cup dairy sour cream and ¼ cup brown sugar (packed). Use remaining cake for another meal.

4 servings.

Hail to the green salad! With endless garnishing possibilities, it's easily the most free-wheeling part of the meal.

For crunch, try thin slices of raw cauliflower, zucchini, mushroom, cucumber, green onion or water chestnuts; thin carrot strips; green pepper or red onion rings; a sprinkle of croutons. For a flavor surprise, take your pick of pickled peppers, mushrooms or beets; olives (ripe or pimiento-stuffed); anchovies; marinated artichoke hearts; bacon bits; cherry tomatoes.

Looking for contrast? Add avocado slices (dipped first in lemon juice), hard-cooked eggs or your choice of cheese: chunks of Cheddar, strips of Swiss, a shake of Parmesan or a crumble of blue.

NEAPOLITAN FEAST

Italian Beef
and Potato Casserole
Tossed Green Salad
Seasoned Breadsticks
Chocolate Ice Cream
Orange-Nut Bars

OVEN SCHEDULE

1 hour 25 minutes before serving:
Bake beef casserole (place on lower rack of oven) and bars (place on upper rack of oven).

15 minutes before serving:
Bake breadsticks (place on upper rack of oven).

If using a larger oven (30-inch), all foods can be baked on one rack.

ITALIAN BEEF
AND POTATO CASSEROLE

1 pound ground beef
1 package (5.5 ounces)
   scalloped potatoes
1 can (16 ounces) tomatoes
1 can (10½ ounces) pizza sauce
1 cup water
½ teaspoon salt
½ teaspoon oregano leaves
¼ teaspoon basil leaves
⅛ teaspoon garlic powder
1 cup creamed cottage cheese
1 package (4 ounces) shredded
   mozzarella cheese
¼ cup grated Parmesan cheese

Heat oven to 350°. In large skillet, cook and stir meat over medium heat until brown. Drain off fat. Stir in sauce mix (from scalloped potatoes), tomatoes, pizza sauce, water, salt, oregano leaves, basil leaves and garlic powder. Heat to boiling, stirring occasionally; remove from heat. Reserve 1 cup meat mixture for topping.

In ungreased 2½-quart casserole, layer half each potato slices, remaining meat mixture, the cottage cheese and mozzarella cheese; repeat. Top with reserved meat mixture; sprinkle with Parmesan cheese. Bake uncovered until liquid is absorbed and potatoes are tender, 1 to 1¼ hours. Let stand 10 minutes before serving.

4 to 6 servings.

SEASONED BREADSTICKS

¼ cup soft butter or margarine
½ teaspoon Italian herb
   seasoning or basil leaves
6 slices white bread

Heat oven to 350°. Mix butter and herb seasoning; spread on one side of bread slices. Cut each slice into 4 sticks; place on ungreased baking sheet. Bake until crisp and golden brown, about 15 minutes.

4 to 6 servings.

ORANGE-NUT BARS

**1 package (14 ounces) orange
  muffin mix**
**½ cup butter or margarine,
  softened**
½ cup brown sugar (packed)
½ cup chopped nuts
½ cup flaked coconut
2 eggs
2 teaspoons grated orange peel
**Confectioners' sugar or ½ cup
  canned vanilla frosting**

Heat oven to 350°. Grease baking pan, 13×9×2 inches. Mix muffin mix and remaining ingredients except confectioners' sugar. Spread in pan. Bake until golden brown and no imprint remains when lightly touched, 20 to 25 minutes. Cool slightly. Sprinkle with confectioners' sugar or spread with frosting; cut into bars, 3×1 inch.

3 dozen bars.

The difference between a crisp, lively tossed salad and one that's limp and soggy may be simply a matter of how you treat the greens. Wash before you store, discarding wilted or discolored leaves. Drain, dry and refrigerate in the crisper, a plastic bag or a covered container. Then for quick work at mealtime, just tear the greens into bite-size pieces with your fingers and toss at the last minute with only enough dressing to coat the leaves.

EASY DOES IT

Steak di Napoli
with Green Beans
Baked Potatoes
Zucchini Toss
Breadsticks
Pineapple Upside-down Ring

Pictured on page 24

OVEN SCHEDULE

2 hours before serving:
 Bake steak (place on lower rack of oven).
1 hour 30 minutes before serving:
 Bake potatoes (place on lower rack of oven).
45 minutes before serving:
 Add green beans and onions to steak.
30 minutes before serving:
 Bake upside-down ring (place on upper rack of oven).
If using a larger oven (30-inch), all foods can be baked on one rack.

STEAK DI NAPOLI
WITH GREEN BEANS

**1½- to 2-pound beef round
 steak, ¾ to 1 inch thick
2 tablespoons flour
1 teaspoon salt
½ teaspoon oregano
¼ teaspoon pepper
1 tablespoon salad oil
1 can (15½ ounces) spaghetti
 sauce with mushrooms
1 package (10 ounces) frozen
 Italian green beans, broken
 apart
1 can (16 ounces) whole
 onions, drained**

Cut meat into 6 pieces. Mix flour, salt, oregano and pepper; coat meat. Heat oil in large skillet; brown meat over medium heat. Drain off fat. If skillet is not ovenproof, transfer meat to ungreased baking dish, 13½×9×2 inches. Pour spaghetti sauce onto meat. Cover and bake in 350° oven 1¼ hours. Add frozen beans and the onions; bake until meat and vegetables are tender, about 45 minutes.

6 servings.

BAKED POTATOES

Heat oven to 350°. Scrub 6 medium baking potatoes, and if softer skins are desired, rub with shortening. Prick with fork to allow steam to escape. Bake until soft, 1¼ to 1½ hours.

To serve, cut crisscross gash in top of each; squeeze gently until some potato pops up through opening. Serve with butter or dairy sour cream.

6 servings.

PINEAPPLE UPSIDE-DOWN RING

¼ cup butter or margarine
1 package (21.5 ounces) pineapple upside-down cake mix
½ cup chilled whipping cream

Heat oven to 350°. In oven, melt butter in 6½-cup anodized ring mold. Sprinkle ½ cup of the topping mix (from cake mix) evenly on butter; top with half the pineapple.

Prepare cake mix as directed on package except—spread batter on topping in ring mold and decrease baking time to 25 to 30 minutes.

Immediately invert cake onto heatproof serving plate; leave pan over cake a minute. In chilled bowl, beat cream and remaining topping mix until stiff; fold in remaining pineapple and serve on warm cake.

6 generous servings.

Red, white or Russet ... which potato should it be for baking? Best known is the long Russet, but there's no hard-and-fast rule. Generally, "old crop" potatoes will bake up mealy and fluffy, whereas early potatoes are waxier—better for boiling and creaming. Mature potatoes will keep for several months stored in a cool, dark, ventilated spot. (In late spring they seem to "do what comes naturally" and start to sprout, no matter how you store them.)

For the Zucchini Toss: Simply add a couple of thinly sliced raw zucchini and any other crispy vegetable you have on hand to your favorite greens and "dress" Italian style. Garnish with ripe olives, green pepper rings and a scatter of croutons.

BAVARIAN BOUNTY

Sauerbraten Stew
with Gingersnap Gravy
Easy Oven Noodles
Mixed Green Salad
Nut-capped Apples

Pictured on page 25

OVEN SCHEDULE

2 hours 40 minutes before serving:
Bake stew (place on lower rack of oven).
1 hour 10 minutes before serving:
Bake apples (place on upper rack of oven).
Add vegetables to stew.
40 minutes before serving:
Bake noodles (place on lower rack of oven).
If using a larger oven (30-inch), all foods can be baked on one
rack.

SAUERBRATEN STEW
WITH GINGERSNAP GRAVY

1½- to 2-pound boneless beef
chuck or sirloin tip roast
1 envelope (4/5 ounce) instant
meat marinade
⅔ cup white vinegar
2 bay leaves
1 teaspoon pickling spice
¼ teaspoon pepper
2 beef bouillon cubes or 2
teaspoons instant beef
bouillon
2½ cups boiling water
5 small onions
5 large carrots, cut diagonally
into 1-inch pieces (about
2 cups)
4 stalks celery, cut diagonally
into 1-inch pieces (about
2 cups)
Gingersnap Gravy (right)

Cut meat into 2-inch pieces. Mix marinade and vinegar in
Dutch oven or 2½-quart casserole; add meat and pierce
pieces with sharp fork. Marinate meat 15 minutes, turning
occasionally.

Stir in bay leaves, pickling spice, pepper, bouillon cubes and
water. Cover and bake in 325° oven until meat is almost
tender, about 1½ hours. Add vegetables; bake until meat
and vegetables are tender, about 1 hour.

Remove meat and vegetables to warm serving dish; keep
warm while making gravy. Pour gravy over meat and
vegetables.

4 servings.

GINGERSNAP GRAVY

Meat broth
¼ cup cold water
2 tablespoons flour
1 teaspoon sugar
⅓ cup crushed gingersnaps (about 6)

Skim fat from broth. Measure broth; if necessary, add enough water to measure 2½ cups. Pour into Dutch oven. Shake ¼ cup water and the flour in covered jar until smooth. Stir into broth. Heat to boiling, stirring constantly. Stir in sugar and gingersnaps. Reduce heat; simmer, stirring occasionally, until gravy is thick and smooth, 3 to 4 minutes.

About 2¾ cups.

EASY OVEN NOODLES

8 ounces uncooked noodles (about 5 cups)
1 teaspoon salt
2 tablespoons butter or salad oil
3½ cups boiling water

Heat oven to 325°. Place noodles in ungreased 1½-quart casserole; sprinkle with salt. Stir butter into water; pour onto noodles. Push noodles into water with spoon. Cover and bake until tender, 35 to 40 minutes.

4 servings.

NUT-CAPPED APPLES

4 baking apples
½ cup raisins
2 tablespoons honey
2 tablespoons chopped pecans
½ cup butterscotch ice-cream topping
½ cup finely chopped pecans

Heat oven to 325°. Core apples; pare upper third of each apple to prevent skin from splitting. Place apples upright in ungreased baking pan, 9×9×2 inches. Mix raisins, honey and 2 tablespoons pecans; fill center of each apple with raisin mixture. Pour hot water into baking pan to ¼-inch depth. Bake until apples are tender when pierced with fork, 50 to 60 minutes (time will vary with size and variety of apple). Cool apples 5 to 10 minutes. Spoon topping onto apples and sprinkle with ½ cup pecans. Or dip upper third of each apple into topping and roll in pecans. Serve warm.

4 servings.

TAMING OF THE STEW

Burgundy Beef Italiano
Mixed Green Salad
Blue Cheese French Bread
Family-style Baked Alaska

OVEN SCHEDULE

3 hours before serving:
Bake beef stew (place on lower rack of oven) and cake (place on upper rack of oven).
20 minutes before serving:
Bake bread (place on upper rack of oven).
3 minutes before serving dessert:
Brown meringue.
If using a larger oven (30-inch), all foods can be baked on one rack.

BURGUNDY BEEF ITALIANO

2 pounds beef stew meat, cut into 1-inch pieces
1 envelope (about 1½ ounces) onion soup mix
1 jar (32 ounces) spaghetti sauce
½ cup red Burgundy
Hot cooked spaghetti

Heat oven to 350°. Mix all ingredients except spaghetti in Dutch oven. Cover and bake until meat is tender, 2½ to 3 hours, stirring occasionally during baking period. (Add small amount of water or Burgundy if necessary.) Serve on spaghetti.

6 servings.

BLUE CHEESE FRENCH BREAD

½ loaf (1-pound size) French bread
¼ cup soft butter or margarine
2 tablespoons crumbled blue cheese
1 tablespoon grated Parmesan cheese

Heat oven to 350°. Cut bread diagonally into 1-inch slices. Mix butter and blue cheese; spread about ⅔ of blue cheese mixture on slices. Reassemble half loaf; spread top with remaining blue cheese mixture and sprinkle with Parmesan cheese. Wrap securely in aluminum foil. Bake 20 minutes.

About 12 slices.

FAMILY-STYLE BAKED ALASKA

6 egg yolks
⅓ cup water
1 package (18.5 ounces) devils food or yellow cake mix
½ gallon peppermint ice cream
6 egg whites
½ teaspoon cream of tartar
1 cup sugar
Chocolate sauce

Heat oven to 350°. Grease and flour baking pan, 13×9×2 inches. Mix egg yolks, water and cake mix. (Batter will be stiff and slightly lumpy.) Spread in pan. Bake 20 minutes. Cool. Place in freezer 1½ hours.

Soften ice cream slightly. Working quickly, spread over chilled cake layer to within ½ inch of edges of pan. Immediately return to freezer while preparing meringue. Beat egg whites and cream of tartar until foamy. Beat in sugar, 1 tablespoon at a time; continue beating until stiff and glossy. Spread meringue on ice cream, sealing it to edges of pan. Return to freezer.

Just before serving, heat oven to 500°. Bake until meringue is light brown, about 3 minutes. Cut half the dessert into six 3-inch squares. (Return remaining dessert to freezer and use the next day.) Serve with chocolate sauce.

6 servings.

Ask someone to name the most glamorous dessert of all, and chances are it will be Baked Alaska. How welcome, then, a recipe so easy you don't have to wait for a super-special occasion: You bake, freeze, brown and serve all in the same pan. It might even be your way of telling the family you think they're special!

It all begins with a chewy, bar-like cake mix base topped with ice cream and sealed under a snowy blanket of meringue. Whisk it into the oven to gild the meringue, then whisk it onto the table for a smashing finish to your dinner. (A sharp knife dipped in hot water makes it a breeze to cut.)

Other match-ups for other times: yellow cake with strawberry ice cream; German chocolate cake with chocolate ice cream; devils food cake with cherry or butterscotch swirl. Sherbet's refreshing, too—try lime sherbet with lemon cake, orange with devils food. And for a final fillip, why not pass around a bowl of your favorite ice-cream topping or sauce? Too good to be true!

GYPSY GOULASH

Easy Oven Ragout
Lettuce Wedges
with Italian Dressing
Herb-Cheese Bread
Individual Lemon-Date Pudding
Cakes

OVEN SCHEDULE

3 hours before serving:
Bake ragout (place on lower rack of oven).
1 hour before serving:
Add potato slices and hot water to ragout.
45 minutes before serving:
Stir ragout.
25 minutes before serving:
Bake bread (place on lower rack of oven) and pudding cakes (place on upper rack of oven).
If using a larger oven (30-inch), all foods can be baked on one rack.

EASY OVEN RAGOUT

1½ to 2 pounds boneless beef stew meat, cut into 1-inch cubes
2 medium onions, cut into eighths
1 cup 1-inch pieces celery
4 medium carrots, cut into 1-inch pieces
1 package (5.5 ounces) scalloped potatoes
1 tablespoon sugar
1 teaspoon salt
½ teaspoon basil leaves
1 can (13½ ounces) tomato juice (about 1⅔ cups)
1 cup hot water

Heat oven to 325°. Mix meat, onions, celery and carrots in ungreased 2½-quart casserole. Sprinkle with sauce mix (from scalloped potatoes), sugar, salt and basil leaves; stir in tomato juice. Cover and bake until meat is almost tender, about 2 hours. Stir in potato slices and hot water; bake 15 minutes. Stir; bake until meat and potatoes are tender, 45 minutes longer.

6 servings.

HERB-CHEESE BREAD

½ loaf (1-pound size) French
 bread
¼ cup soft butter or margarine
1 teaspoon snipped parsley
¼ teaspoon oregano leaves or
 basil leaves
1 tablespoon grated Parmesan
 cheese
Dash garlic salt

Heat oven to 325°. Cut bread diagonally into 1-inch slices. Mix remaining ingredients; spread on slices. Reassemble half loaf and wrap securely in aluminum foil. Bake 25 minutes.

About 12 slices.

INDIVIDUAL LEMON-DATE PUDDING CAKES

1 can (22 ounces) lemon pie
 filling
½ cup chopped dates
½ package (18.5-ounce size)
 lemon or yellow cake mix*
⅔ cup water
1 egg
Whipped cream or ice cream

Heat oven to 325°. Divide pie filling evenly among 6 greased 10-ounce custard cups or baking dishes. Sprinkle dates on pie filling in each cup (about 1 tablespoon in each).

In small mixer bowl, blend cake mix, water and egg on low speed ½ minute, scraping bowl constantly. Beat on medium speed 3 minutes, scraping bowl occasionally. Divide evenly among custard cups. Place cups on baking sheet. Bake until wooden pick inserted in center of cake comes out clean, about 25 minutes. Serve in cups, or just before serving, invert onto dessert plates. Serve warm, topped with whipped cream.

6 servings.

*To measure ½ package cake mix, pour contents of package into a bowl. Fluff mix with fork and spoon lightly into a measuring cup to determine total quantity. Divide in half (about 2¼ cups). Store the unused mix in package, folding down the inner liner tightly. For best results, opened package should be used within 2 weeks.

NOTE: If custard cups are not available, spread pie filling and dates in ungreased baking pan, 9×9×2 inches, and place in oven until hot, about 10 minutes. Pour batter onto filling and increase baking time to 35 to 40 minutes. Spoon into dessert dishes.

BIG BEEF

Savory Pot Roast
with Sour Cream Gravy
Hot French Bread
Lettuce Wedges with Favorite
Dressing
Raspberry Sherbet

OVEN SCHEDULE

3 hours before serving:
    Bake pot roast (place on lower rack of oven).
1½ hours before serving:
    Add carrots to roast.
40 minutes before serving:
    Add onions and Brussels sprouts to roast.
15 minutes before serving:
    Heat foil-wrapped French bread (place on upper rack of oven).
If using a larger oven (30-inch), all foods can be baked on one rack.

SAVORY POT ROAST WITH SOUR CREAM GRAVY

2 tablespoons salad oil
3-pound beef pot roast
1 cup water
1 bay leaf
¼ teaspoon marjoram leaves
¼ teaspoon celery seed
6 to 8 medium carrots, cut into 3-inch lengths, then each length cut diagonally
6 small onions
1 package (10 ounces) frozen Brussels sprouts, partially thawed
½ teaspoon salt
1 cup dairy sour cream
1 tablespoon flour
½ teaspoon salt
½ teaspoon paprika

Heat oil in Dutch oven; brown meat over medium heat, about 15 minutes. Drain off fat. Add water, bay leaf, marjoram leaves and celery seed. Cover and bake in 325° oven 1½ hours. Add carrots; bake until meat and carrots are almost tender, about 1 hour. Add onions and Brussels sprouts; sprinkle with ½ teaspoon salt and bake until meat and vegetables are tender, 30 to 40 minutes.

Remove meat and vegetables to warm platter; keep warm while making gravy. Skim fat from meat broth. Measure broth; if necessary, add enough water to measure 1 cup. Mix sour cream, flour, ½ teaspoon salt and the paprika in Dutch oven. Stir in meat broth gradually and heat to boiling, stirring constantly.

6 servings.

Menus pictured on the following pages: Individual Barbecued Meat Loaves (pages 6-7), Steak di Napoli (pages 14-15), Sauerbraten Stew (pages 16-17), Gingered Ham Slice (pages 32-33)

BEEF-EATER'S DELIGHT

Roast Beef au Jus
with Oven-browned Potatoes
Cauliflower-Sprouts au Gratin
Tomatoes Vinaigrette
Steamed Date Pudding

OVEN SCHEDULE

3 hours before serving:
Bake roast beef (place on lower rack of oven)—time is approximate and may be less, depending on type and weight of roast.

2 hours before serving:
Bake pudding (place on lower rack of oven).

1 hour 15 minutes before serving:
Add potatoes to roast beef.

1 hour before serving:
Bake vegetable casserole (place on upper rack of oven).

If using a larger oven (30-inch), all foods can be baked on one rack.

ROAST BEEF AU JUS WITH OVEN-BROWNED POTATOES

Select roast from those listed in timetable on page 30. Allow about ½ pound per person. If desired, season roast with salt and pepper before, during or after roasting (salt goes into the meat only ¼ to ½ inch). Place meat fat side up on rack in shallow roasting pan. It is not necessary to baste; with the fat on top, the meat does its own basting. Insert meat thermometer so tip is in thickest part of meat and does not rest in fat. Roast meat uncovered in 325° oven to desired doneness (see timetable), using thermometer reading as final guide.

About 1½ hours before roast is done, pare 6 medium baking potatoes. If you wish, make thin crosswise cuts almost through potatoes. Heat 1 inch salted water (½ teaspoon salt to 1 cup water) to boiling in saucepan. Add potatoes. Cover and heat to boiling; cook 10 minutes. Drain.

Place potatoes in meat drippings in roasting pan; turn each potato to coat with fat. Or brush potatoes with melted butter or margarine and place on rack with meat. *(continued)*

Turning once, bake until tender and golden brown, about 1¼ hours. Season with salt and pepper.

Roast beef is easier to carve if allowed to set for 15 to 20 minutes after removing from oven. Since meat continues to cook after removal from oven, if roast is to set, it should be removed from oven when thermometer registers 5 to 10° lower than the desired temperature. To serve "au jus," spoon meat juices onto the meat slices.

Timetable

Cut	Approximate Weight	Meat Thermometer Reading	Approximate Cooking Time (minutes per lb.)	Total Cooking Time
Rolled Rib	4 pounds	140 to 160°	32 to 38	About 2 hours to 2 hours 30 minutes
Rolled Rump (high quality)	4 pounds	150 to 170°	25 to 30	1 hour 40 minutes to 2 hours
Sirloin Tip (high quality)	4 pounds	150 to 170°	35 to 40	2 hours 20 minutes to 2 hours 40 minutes

CAULIFLOWER-SPROUTS AU GRATIN

1 package (10 ounces) frozen cauliflower, thawed
1 package (10 ounces) frozen Brussels sprouts, thawed
1 can (10¾ ounces) condensed Cheddar cheese soup
1 tablespoon instant minced onion
½ teaspoon salt
¼ teaspoon dry mustard
Dash white pepper

Heat oven to 325°. Combine cauliflower and Brussels sprouts in ungreased 1-quart casserole. Mix soup and seasonings; pour onto vegetables. Cover and bake until bubbly, 50 to 60 minutes.

6 servings.

STEAMED DATE PUDDING

½ cup hot water
1 package (14 ounces) date bar
　mix
2 eggs
½ cup finely chopped nuts
½ cup currants or raisins
½ teaspoon mace
½ teaspoon cinnamon
¼ teaspoon nutmeg
Amber Sauce (below) or
　favorite sauce

AMBER SAUCE

½ cup brown sugar (packed) or
　granulated sugar
¼ cup light corn syrup
¼ cup light cream
2 tablespoons butter or
　margarine

Heat oven to 325°. Mix water and date filling (from date bar mix). Stir in crumbly mix, eggs, nuts, currants, mace, cinnamon and nutmeg. Pour into well-greased 4-cup mold or casserole. Cover mold with aluminum foil.

Place mold on rack in Dutch oven; pour hot water into Dutch oven to ½ the depth of mold and heat to boiling. Cover and bake 2 hours. Uncover pudding and let stand at room temperature about 5 minutes. Unmold onto serving plate. Serve warm, with Amber Sauce.

6 generous servings.

Cook all ingredients in small saucepan over low heat 5 minutes, stirring occasionally. Serve warm.

1 cup.

No need to cross steamed pudding off your menu because you don't own a steamer. This one is _oven_ steamed—and made easy with date bar mix besides.

For a traditional hard sauce, soften ½ cup butter or margarine and blend well with 1 cup confectioners' sugar and 2 teaspoons vanilla. Then for the traditional dramatic finale, dim the lights and flame the pudding: Heat about ¼ cup brandy in a tiny long-handled pan (a butter-melter or what-have-you). Ignite with a kitchen or fireplace match and pour flaming over the unmolded pudding. No brandy? Soak enough sugar cubes to surround the unmolded pudding in lemon extract. The cubes needn't touch; by lighting just one cube, flames will magically encircle the pudding.

Any leftover pudding can be wrapped in aluminum foil and reheated in a 350° oven for about 20 minutes.

JUST PEACHY

Corned Beef and Peaches
Scalloped Potatoes Deluxe
Baked Cabbage Slaw
Raw Vegetable Relishes
Gingerbread with Lemon Sauce

OVEN SCHEDULE

4 hours before serving:
Bake corned beef (place on lower rack of oven).
1 hour before serving:
Bake scalloped potatoes (place on lower rack of oven) and cabbage slaw (place on upper rack of oven).
35 minutes before serving:
Bake gingerbread (place on upper rack of oven).
Add glaze and peaches to corned beef.
If using a larger oven (30-inch), all foods can be baked on one rack.

CORNED BEEF AND PEACHES

2½- to 3-pound **well-trimmed corned beef brisket**
2 teaspoons **whole pickling spice**
¼ cup **brown sugar (packed)**
¼ cup **prepared mustard**
1 can (29 ounces) **cling peach halves, drained (reserve ¼ cup syrup)**

Place meat and pickling spice in Dutch oven; cover with hot water. Cover and bake in 325° oven until tender, about 3½ hours. Drain off liquid. Mix brown sugar, mustard and reserved peach syrup; pour onto meat. Arrange peach halves around meat and bake uncovered 30 minutes. To serve, cut meat into thin slices across grain at a slanted angle. Garnish with peach halves and serve with remaining pan juices.

6 servings.

Even though this hearty dinner calls for corned beef brisket, should your meat man be featuring corned beef round, you may find that particular cut leaner and perhaps less expensive. Cooking times are about the same—but look on the label for special baking directions with either cut. As for the pickling spice: If you buy corned beef mildly cured, add the amount the recipe calls for; if it's already highly spiced, go easy. With some brands you get a packet of pickling spice with the meat.

SCALLOPED POTATOES DELUXE

Heat oven to 325°. Prepare 1 package (5.5 ounces) scalloped potatoes as directed except—stir in 1 can (3 ounces) sliced mushrooms, drained, and bake 1 hour.

6 servings.

BAKED CABBAGE SLAW

4 cups coarsely shredded green cabbage
1 can (16 ounces) cut green beans, drained
¼ cup sugar
1 small onion, sliced
1 teaspoon salt
½ cup vinegar

Heat oven to 325°. Combine all ingredients in ungreased 2-quart casserole. Cover and bake until cabbage is crisp-tender and beans are hot, 50 to 60 minutes.

6 servings.

GINGERBREAD WITH LEMON SAUCE

1 package (14.5 ounces) gingerbread mix
1 cup lukewarm water
½ cup finely chopped walnuts or pecans (optional)
Lemon Sauce (below) or favorite lemon sauce

Heat oven to 325°. Grease and flour baking pan, 9×9×2 inches. In large mixer bowl, blend gingerbread mix and water on low speed, scraping bowl constantly. Beat on medium speed 2 minutes, scraping bowl occasionally, or beat 300 strokes by hand. Stir in nuts. Pour into pan. Bake until wooden pick inserted in center comes out clean, 30 to 35 minutes. Cut 6 servings from cake; serve warm, with sauce. Use remaining cake for another meal.

6 servings.

LEMON SAUCE

½ cup sugar
1 tablespoon cornstarch
1 cup water
1 tablespoon butter or margarine
1 tablespoon grated lemon peel
1 tablespoon lemon juice

In small saucepan, mix sugar and cornstarch. Stir in water. Cook, stirring constantly, until mixture thickens and boils. Boil and stir 1 minute. Stir in remaining ingredients. Serve warm.

About 1 cup.

ANY WAY YOU SLICE IT

Gingered Ham Slice
Oven-steamed Rice
Brussels Sprouts and Carrots
Spinach-Avocado-Orange Salad
Rye Rolls
Chocolate-Banana Shortcake

Pictured on page 26

OVEN SCHEDULE

40 minutes before serving:
Bake vegetables and shortcake (place on upper rack of oven).
30 minutes before serving:
Bake ham (place on lower rack of oven) and rice (place on upper rack of oven).
10 minutes before serving:
Heat foil-wrapped rolls (place on lower rack of oven).
If using a larger oven (30-inch), all foods can be baked on one rack.

GINGERED HAM SLICE

**1 fully cooked smoked ham
slice, 1 inch thick
¼ cup ginger marmalade**

Place ham slice in ungreased baking pan, 13×9×2 inches; brush with marmalade. Bake in 350° oven until hot, about 30 minutes, brushing ham once with marmalade during baking period.

4 servings.

VARIATION
Curried Ham Slice: Substitute a mixture of 3 tablespoons butter or margarine, melted, 2 tablespoons wine vinegar, 2 teaspoons curry powder and ½ teaspoon dry mustard for the ginger marmalade.

OVEN-STEAMED RICE

**2 cups boiling water
1 cup uncooked regular rice
1 teaspoon salt**

Heat oven to 350°. Mix all ingredients in ungreased 1- or 1½-quart casserole. Cover tightly and bake until liquid is absorbed and rice is tender, about 30 minutes.

4 servings.

BRUSSELS SPROUTS AND CARROTS

1 package (10 ounces) frozen
   Brussels sprouts, partially
   thawed
1 can (16 ounces) small whole
   carrots, drained
2 tablespoons butter or
   margarine, melted
2 teaspoons lemon juice
½ teaspoon salt

Heat oven to 350°. Combine Brussels sprouts and carrots in ungreased 1- to 1½-quart casserole. Cover and bake until Brussels sprouts are tender, 35 to 40 minutes. Mix butter, lemon juice and salt; drizzle on vegetables.

4 servings.

CHOCOLATE-BANANA SHORTCAKE

1⅓ cups buttermilk baking mix
½ cup sugar
⅓ cup cocoa
1 egg
⅔ cup milk
3 tablespoons butter or
   margarine, softened
Sweetened whipped cream or
   vanilla ice cream
1 banana, sliced

Heat oven to 350°. Grease and flour baking pan, 8×8×2 inches. In large mixer bowl, blend all ingredients except whipped cream and banana on low speed ½ minute, scraping bowl frequently. Beat on medium speed 4 minutes, scraping bowl occasionally. Pour into pan. Bake until wooden pick inserted in center comes out clean, 30 to 35 minutes. Cut 4 servings from cake. Serve warm, topped with whipped cream and banana slices. Use remaining cake for another meal.

4 servings.

NOTE: If you're pressed for time, bake Cake-like Brownies as directed on 1 package (15.5 ounces) fudge brownie mix. Cut 4 servings from the brownies. Serve warm, topped with whipped cream and banana slices. Use remaining brownies for another meal.

VARIATION
Spiced Chocolate-Banana Shortcake: Add 1 teaspoon cinnamon to ingredients before blending. Stir ½ teaspoon cinnamon into ½ cup chocolate syrup; drizzle on whipped cream and banana slices.

HAM IT UP

Ham Loaf Superb
Hot Mustard Fruits
Baked Sweet Potatoes
Spinach Provençale
Broccoli Buds, Cauliflowerets,
Radish Fans
Butterscotch Chiffon Pudding

OVEN SCHEDULE

1 hour 25 minutes before serving:
Bake ham loaf (place on lower rack of oven).
50 minutes before serving:
Bake sweet potatoes (place on lower rack of oven)
25 minutes before serving:
Bake fruits and spinach (place on upper rack of oven).
3 minutes before serving:
Bake cheese-topped loaf.
If using a larger oven (30-inch), all foods can be baked on one rack.

HAM LOAF SUPERB

1 pound ground ham
**½ pound ground veal or
ground beef**
½ pound ground lean pork
2 eggs, beaten
1 cup quick-cooking oats
¾ cup tomato juice
⅓ cup finely chopped onion
1 teaspoon salt
¼ teaspoon pepper
**4 square slices mozzarella,
American or Swiss cheese,
cut diagonally into triangles**

Mix all ingredients except cheese thoroughly. In ungreased baking pan, 13×9×2 inches, shape mixture into loaf, 9×5×3 inches. Bake in 350° oven until brown, 1 to 1¼ hours. Remove from oven; let stand a few minutes, then transfer ham loaf to ovenproof platter. Make slits about ⅓ of the way through loaf at 1-inch intervals and insert a cheese triangle long side down in each. Place loaf in oven until cheese is slightly melted, 2 to 3 minutes.

6 servings.

HOT MUSTARD FRUITS

1 can (16 ounces) sliced
  peaches, drained
1 can (13½ ounces) pineapple
  tidbits, drained
2 bananas, cut into 1-inch
  pieces
¼ cup butter or margarine,
  melted
½ cup brown sugar (packed)
2 tablespoons prepared
  mustard

Heat oven to 350°. Combine fruits in ungreased 1½-quart casserole. Mix butter, brown sugar and mustard thoroughly; reserve 2 tablespoons for topping. Pour remaining mustard mixture onto fruits and toss. Spoon reserved mustard mixture on top. Bake uncovered until fruits are hot, 20 to 25 minutes.

6 servings.

BAKED SWEET POTATOES

Heat oven to 350°. Scrub 6 medium sweet potatoes, and if soft skins are desired, rub with small amount shortening. Prick with fork to allow steam to escape. Bake until soft, about 50 minutes.

To serve, cut crisscross gash in each potato; squeeze gently until some potato pops up through opening. Dot with butter and sprinkle with salt and pepper.

6 servings.

SPINACH PROVENCALE

2 packages (10 ounces each)
  frozen leaf spinach
2 eggs
1 tablespoon flour
1 teaspoon salt
⅛ teaspoon pepper
½ teaspoon lemon juice
2 tablespoons finely chopped
  onion
2 slices bread, buttered and
  cubed

Heat oven to 350°. Cook spinach as directed on package except—omit salt. Drain. In large bowl, beat eggs, flour, salt, pepper and lemon juice with rotary beater until smooth. Add onion and spinach and toss. Turn into buttered 1-quart casserole. Sprinkle with bread cubes. Bake uncovered until bread cubes are golden brown, 20 to 25 minutes.

6 servings.

COUNTRY CUPBOARD

Glazed Baked Ham
Easy Oven Squash
Herbed Peas and Celery
Creamy Coleslaw
Pineapple Bread Pudding

OVEN SCHEDULE

2 hours 35 minutes before serving:
Bake ham (place on lower rack of oven).
1 hour 15 minutes before serving:
Bake squash (place on lower rack of oven).
45 minutes before serving:
Bake pudding and peas and celery (place on upper rack of oven).
30 minutes before serving:
Glaze ham.
20 minutes before serving:
Stir onion into squash.
If using a larger oven (30-inch), all foods can be baked on one rack.

GLAZED BAKED HAM

Place 5-pound smoked picnic shoulder (fully cooked) fat side up on rack in shallow roasting pan. Insert meat thermometer so tip is in thickest part of meat and does not touch bone or rest in fat. Bake uncovered in 325° oven until done, about 2 hours 15 minutes, or until thermometer registers 130°.

About 30 minutes before ham is done, remove from oven. Drain off fat. Score fat surface of ham lightly, cutting uniform diamond shapes. If desired, insert whole clove in each diamond. Mix ¼ cup honey, ½ teaspoon dry mustard and ¼ teaspoon cloves; spoon or spread on ham and bake 30 minutes.

Ham is easier to carve if allowed to set for 15 to 20 minutes after removing from oven. Since meat continues to cook after removal from oven, if ham is to set, it should be removed from oven when thermometer registers 5° lower than desired temperature.

EASY OVEN SQUASH

2 packages (10 ounces each)
  frozen cooked squash
½ teaspoon salt
2 tablespoons butter or
  margarine
2 tablespoons instant minced
  onion or ¼ cup finely
  chopped onion

Heat oven to 325°. Place frozen squash in ungreased 1½-quart casserole. Sprinkle with salt and dot with butter. Cover and bake 55 minutes. Stir in onion and bake until squash is hot, about 20 minutes. Stir before serving.

4 to 6 servings.

HERBED PEAS AND CELERY

1 package (10 ounces) frozen
  green peas
1 cup thinly sliced celery
½ teaspoon salt
¼ teaspoon basil leaves
2 tablespoons butter or
  margarine

Heat oven to 325°. Rinse peas with small amount of running cold water to separate and remove ice crystals; drain. Place peas and celery in ungreased 1-quart casserole. Sprinkle with salt and basil leaves and dot with butter. Cover and bake until vegetables are tender, 40 to 45 minutes. Stir before serving.

4 to 6 servings.

PINEAPPLE BREAD PUDDING

½ cup butter or margarine,
  softened
1 cup sugar
½ teaspoon cinnamon
4 eggs
1 can (13½ ounces) crushed
  pineapple, well drained
2 cups ½-inch bread cubes
  (about 3 slices)
¼ cup chopped pecans

Heat oven to 325°. In large mixer bowl, beat butter, sugar and cinnamon on medium speed 1 minute, scraping bowl constantly. Add eggs; scraping bowl occasionally, beat on high speed until mixture is light and fluffy, 2 minutes. Fold in pineapple, bread cubes and pecans. Pour into greased 1½-quart casserole. Bake until knife inserted in center comes out clean, 40 to 45 minutes.

4 to 6 servings.

PROVINCIAL POTLUCK

Baked Bean Cassoulet
Brown Bread
Tomato Coleslaw
Lemon-glazed Apple Pies

OVEN SCHEDULE

3 hours 30 minutes before serving:
Bake cassoulet (place on lower rack of oven).
1 hour before serving:
Uncover cassoulet.
30 minutes before serving:
Bake bread (place on lower rack of oven) and pies (place on upper rack of oven).
If using a larger oven (30-inch), all foods can be baked on one rack.

BAKED BEAN CASSOULET

1 cup dried kidney beans (about ½ pound)
1 cup dried pinto beans (about ½ pound)
¾ pound Italian link sausages or pork link sausages, cut into 1-inch pieces
½ pound cooked ham, cut into ½-inch cubes
1 medium onion, sliced
¼ cup molasses
1 can (15 ounces) tomato sauce
1 teaspoon salt
¼ teaspoon dry mustard
⅛ teaspoon pepper
1 tablespoon Worcestershire sauce

Place beans in large saucepan and cover with water. Heat to boiling; boil 2 minutes. Remove from heat; cover and let stand 1 hour.

Add water if necessary to cover beans and simmer uncovered until tender, about 50 minutes. (Do not boil or beans will burst.) Drain; reserve liquid.

Heat oven to 300°. Layer beans, meat and onion in ungreased 2½-quart bean pot or casserole. Mix remaining ingredients and 1 cup of the reserved bean liquid; pour onto beans. Add enough of the remaining reserved liquid or water to almost cover beans. Cover and bake 2½ hours. Uncover and bake 1 hour longer. Stir beans if they look dry during baking.

6 servings.

NOTE: If you prefer, soak beans in cold water overnight. Heat beans in same water to boiling; simmer until tender, 1 to 2 hours. Drain; reserve liquid. Bake as directed.

BROWN BREAD

Heat oven to 300°. Remove brown bread (16 ounces) from can. Cut into ½-inch slices. Reassemble loaf and wrap in aluminum foil. Place on ungreased baking sheet. Bake 30 minutes.

6 servings.

LEMON-GLAZED APPLE PIES

6 commercially baked
  individual apple pies
1 cup confectioners' sugar
1 teaspoon grated lemon peel
2 tablespoons lemon juice

Heat oven to 300°. Place pies on ungreased baking sheet. Bake 30 minutes. Mix sugar, lemon peel and lemon juice until smooth; spread on warm pies and serve.

6 servings.

Too busy for pot-watching? Let your oven "mind" this old-fashioned casserole. Then half an hour before sit-down, fix the rest of the meal.

For the slaw: Shred or chop about half a medium head of cabbage and half an onion.

Blend ½ cup dairy sour cream and ¼ cup mayonnaise or salad dressing with seasoned salt, dry mustard and pepper to taste. Toss with the cabbage and onion. For each serving, top chubby slices of tomato with the slaw; rosy it all up with a sprinkle of paprika.

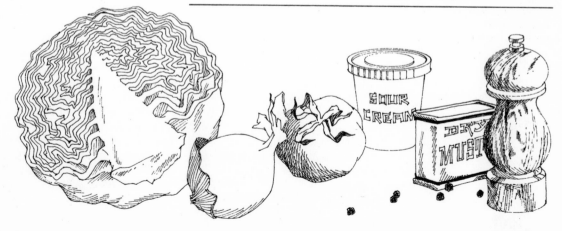

GERMAN ACCENT

Pork Chops and Sauerkraut
Savory Peas and Limas
Celery Fans and Carrot Sticks
Caraway Rye Rolls
Spiced Apple Upside-down
Cake

Pictured on page 51

OVEN SCHEDULE

1 hour 30 minutes before serving:
　　Bake pork chop casserole (place on lower rack of oven).
50 minutes before serving:
　　Bake peas and limas (place on lower rack of oven).
40 minutes before serving:
　　Bake cake (place on upper rack of oven).
10 minutes before serving:
　　Heat foil-wrapped rolls (place on lower rack of oven).
If using a larger oven (30-inch), all foods can be baked on one rack.

PORK CHOPS AND SAUERKRAUT

1 can (16 ounces) sauerkraut
½ cup water
¾ cup chopped onion
2 tablespoons uncooked barley
½ teaspoon salt
½ cup catsup
2 teaspoons Worcestershire sauce
4 to 6 loin or rib pork chops, ¾ inch thick

Heat oven to 350°. Mix sauerkraut (with liquid), water, onion, barley and salt in ungreased 2-quart casserole or baking dish, 11¾×7½×1½ inches. Mix catsup and Worcestershire sauce in small shallow dish. Coat chops with catsup mixture and place on sauerkraut. Cover and bake until chops are tender, 1¼ to 1½ hours.

4 servings.

Bake frozen vegetables along with the rest of the meal—it's easy, does good things to the flavor and preserves nutrients. Almost any vegetable is a likely candidate: Simply place the frozen block with 1 to 2 tablespoons butter or margarine and ¼ teaspoon salt in a casserole. (For lima beans add 2 tablespoons water.) Cover; bake 40 to 55 minutes at 350° or 50 to 65 minutes at 325°. Stir 15 minutes before the cooking time is up.

SAVORY PEAS AND LIMAS

1 package (10 ounces) frozen
green peas
1 package (10 ounces) frozen
lima beans
½ teaspoon salt
¼ teaspoon savory
¼ teaspoon dry mustard
2 tablespoons water
2 tablespoons butter or
margarine

Heat oven to 350°. Rinse peas and beans with small amount of running cold water to separate and remove ice crystals; drain. Place in ungreased 1-quart casserole. Sprinkle with salt, savory, mustard and water; dot with butter. Cover and bake until vegetables are tender, about 50 minutes. Stir vegetables before serving.

4 servings.

SPICED APPLE UPSIDE-DOWN CAKE

¼ cup butter or margarine
½ cup brown sugar (packed)
1 jar (14 ounces) spiced apple
rings, drained
½ package (18.5-ounce size)
yellow or honey spice cake
mix*
⅔ cup water
1 egg
Sweetened whipped cream or
ice cream

Heat oven to 350°. In oven, melt butter in baking pan, 8×8×2 or 9×9×2 inches, or layer pan, 9×1½ inches. Sprinkle brown sugar on butter. Cut apple rings into halves and arrange on brown sugar.

In small mixer bowl, blend cake mix, water and egg on low speed ½ minute, scraping bowl constantly. Beat on medium speed 3 minutes, scraping bowl occasionally. Pour onto fruit. Bake until wooden pick inserted in center comes out clean, 35 to 40 minutes. Invert onto serving plate; leave pan over cake a few minutes. Cut 4 servings from cake. Serve warm, with whipped cream. Use remaining cake for another meal.

4 servings.

*To measure ½ package cake mix, pour contents of package into a bowl. Fluff mix with fork and spoon lightly into a measuring cup to determine total quantity. Divide in half (about 2¼ cups). Store the unused mix in package, folding down the inner liner tightly. For best results, opened package should be used within 2 weeks.

VARIATION

Apricot-Prune Upside-down Cake: Substitute 16 cooked apricot halves and 16 pitted cooked prunes, arranged alternately in checkerboard design on brown sugar, for the spiced apple rings.

SAY CHEESE!

Stuffed Pork Chops Gruyère
Crunchy Corn Bake
Tomatoes Vinaigrette
Cherry-Berry Streusel

OVEN SCHEDULE

1 hour 30 minutes before serving:
    Bake pork chops (place on lower rack of oven).
40 minutes before serving:
    Bake corn casserole and dessert (place on upper rack of oven).
If using a larger oven (30-inch), all foods can be baked on one rack.

STUFFED PORK CHOPS GRUYERE

2 cups soft bread cubes
1 cup shredded Gruyère cheese (about 4 ounces)
¼ cup chopped green onion
¼ cup milk
1 egg, beaten
6 rib pork chops, 1 inch thick (with pockets cut into chops)
2 tablespoons salad oil
1 teaspoon garlic salt
½ teaspoon salt
¼ teaspoon pepper
½ cup water

Mix bread cubes, cheese, onion, milk and egg. Stuff pork chop pockets with cheese mixture. Heat oil in large skillet; brown chops over medium heat, about 15 minutes. If skillet is not ovenproof, transfer chops to ungreased baking dish, 13½×9×2 inches. Sprinkle garlic salt, salt and pepper on chops; pour in water. Cover and bake in 350° oven until tender, 1¼ to 1½ hours.

6 servings.

CRUNCHY CORN BAKE

2 cans (12 ounces each) whole kernel corn, drained
½ cup chopped celery
½ teaspoon celery salt
⅛ teaspoon pepper
2 tablespoons butter or margarine

Heat oven to 350°. Place corn and celery in ungreased 1½-quart casserole. Sprinkle with seasonings and dot with butter. Cover and bake until corn is hot, about 40 minutes. Stir before serving.

6 servings.

CHERRY-BERRY STREUSEL

1 can (21 ounces) cherry pie filling
1 can (15 ounces) blueberries, drained (reserve ¼ cup liquid)
½ package (18.5-ounce size) yellow cake mix*
⅔ cup water
1 egg
Streusel Topping (below)

Heat oven to 350°. Mix pie filling, blueberries and reserved blueberry liquid in ungreased baking dish, 11¾×7½×1½ inches, or baking pan, 9×9×2 inches.

In small mixer bowl, blend cake mix, water and egg on low speed ½ minute, scraping bowl constantly. Beat on medium speed 3 minutes, scraping bowl occasionally. Pour onto fruit; sprinkle with Streusel Topping. Bake until wooden pick inserted in center of cake comes out clean, about 40 minutes. Cut into squares or spoon into dessert dishes, and if desired, top with ice cream or whipped topping. Serve warm.

6 generous servings.

*To measure ½ package cake mix, pour contents of package into a bowl. Fluff mix with fork and spoon lightly into a measuring cup to determine total quantity. Divide in half (about 2¼ cups). Store the unused mix in package, folding down the inner liner tightly. For best results, use opened package within 2 weeks.

STREUSEL TOPPING

⅓ cup sugar
⅓ cup all-purpose flour
¾ teaspoon cinnamon
¼ cup soft butter or margarine

Mix all ingredients with fork until crumbly.

About ¾ cup.

It takes an extra-thick chop to make the elegant cheese-stuffed pork chops that star in this dinner. Even if the chops come already packaged, an accommodating meat man will usually cut pockets in them for you. If the pockets are cut from the rib sides of the chops, they will close up during cooking, sealing in the bread-cheese stuffing. Or you can fasten the pockets with wooden picks or small skewers, removing them just before serving.

Don't despair if Gruyère cheese is not available. Although they're milder and less tangy in flavor, such cheeses as Swiss, Monterey Jack or mozzarella will do nicely for the stuffing.

HEARTY HOSPITALITY

Stuffed Pork Tenderloin
Spiced Apricots
Green Bean Casserole
Tomato Aspic Molds
Apple-Mince Pie a la Mode

OVEN SCHEDULE

1 hour 30 minutes before serving:
   Bake pork tenderloin (place on upper rack of oven) and pie (place on lower rack of oven).
40 minutes before serving:
   Bake bean casserole (place on upper rack of oven).
5 minutes before serving:
   Sprinkle noodles on bean casserole.
If using a larger oven (30-inch), all foods can be baked on one rack.

STUFFED PORK TENDERLOIN

2 pork tenderloins (¾ to 1 pound each)
Salt and pepper
Bread Stuffing (below) or favorite stuffing
4 to 6 slices bacon

Make a cut lengthwise in center of each tenderloin, being careful not to cut completely through. Spread tenderloins open. Place one cut side up; season with salt and pepper and spread with stuffing. Place other tenderloin cut side down on top and tie with string. Place on rack in shallow roasting pan. Arrange bacon slices on meat. Bake uncovered in 350° oven until done, 1¼ to 1½ hours.

4 to 6 servings.

BREAD STUFFING

⅓ cup butter or margarine
¼ cup finely chopped onion
½ cup chopped celery (stalk and leaves)
3 cups soft bread cubes
½ teaspoon salt
½ teaspoon crushed sage leaves
¼ teaspoon thyme leaves
⅛ teaspoon pepper

Melt butter in large skillet. Cook and stir onion and celery in butter until onion is tender. Stir in about 1 cup of the bread cubes. Turn into bowl; add remaining ingredients and toss.

3 cups.

GREEN BEAN CASSEROLE

2 packages (9 ounces each) frozen cut green beans or French-style green beans
1 can (16 ounces) bean sprouts, rinsed and drained
1 can (10½ ounces) condensed golden mushroom, cream of celery or cream of chicken soup
1 teaspoon salt
1 teaspoon soy sauce
1 can (3 ounces) chow mein noodles (about 2 cups) or 1 cup canned French fried onions

Heat oven to 350°. Rinse beans with small amount of running cold water to separate and remove ice crystals; drain. Mix beans, bean sprouts, soup, salt and soy sauce. Turn into ungreased baking dish, 11¾×7½×1½ inches. Bake uncovered 35 minutes. Sprinkle noodles on top and bake 5 minutes.

4 to 6 servings.

APPLE-MINCE PIE A LA MODE

Pastry for 9-inch two-crust pie
1 tablespoon finely shredded orange peel
½ jar (28-ounce size) prepared mincemeat flavored with brandy and rum (1⅓ cups)
1 can (20 ounces) unsweetened apple slices
½ cup chopped walnuts
2 tablespoons sugar
Vanilla ice cream or hard sauce

Heat oven to 350°. Prepare pastry as directed in your favorite recipe or on 1 package (11 ounces) pie crust sticks or mix except—stir orange peel into flour or dry mix.

Mix mincemeat, apple slices and walnuts. Turn into pastry-lined pie pan. Cover with top crust that has slits cut in it; seal and flute. Brush crust with water and sprinkle sugar on top. Cover edge with 2- to 3-inch-wide strip of aluminum foil to prevent excessive browning; remove foil last 15 minutes of baking. Bake until crust is brown and juice begins to bubble through slits in crust, about 70 minutes. Serve warm, with ice cream.

STICK TO THE RIBS

Spiced Spareribs and Apples
Baked Acorn Squash
Buttered Green Beans
Green Pepper Slaw
German Chocolate Brownies

Pictured on page 52

OVEN SCHEDULE

2 hours 30 minutes before serving:
Bake spareribs (place on lower rack of oven) and brownies (place on upper rack of oven).

1 hour before serving:
Bake squash (place on upper rack of oven).

45 minutes before serving:
Bake green beans (place on upper rack of oven).

30 minutes before serving:
Uncover spareribs.

15 minutes before serving:
Turn and season squash.
Stir green beans.

If using a larger oven (30-inch), all foods can be baked on one rack.

SPICED SPARERIBS AND APPLES

Two 2-pound strips spareribs
2 teaspoons salt
½ teaspoon pepper
½ teaspoon allspice
3 medium baking apples, cut into ½-inch wedges
2 tablespoons brown sugar
½ teaspoon allspice
3 cups apple cider
¼ cup cinnamon apple jelly

Place 1 strip spareribs meaty side down on rack in large roasting pan. Mix salt, pepper and ½ teaspoon allspice; sprinkle half the mixture on spareribs in pan. Layer apples on spareribs; sprinkle with brown sugar. Place remaining strip spareribs meaty side up on apples. Stir ½ teaspoon allspice into cider; pour onto spareribs. Sprinkle with remaining salt mixture. Cover and bake in 350° oven 2 hours. Uncover and bake until spareribs are tender, about ½ hour, basting with cider 2 or 3 times during the baking period. Melt jelly over low heat; brush on spareribs.

4 servings.

BAKED ACORN SQUASH

Heat oven to 350°. Cut 2 medium acorn squash in half; remove seeds and fibers. Place squash cut sides down in ungreased baking dish, 11¾×7½×1½ inches. Pour boiling water into baking dish to ¼-inch depth. Bake uncovered 45 minutes. Turn; season with salt and pepper and dot with butter. Bake until tender, about 15 minutes.

4 servings.

BUTTERED GREEN BEANS

1 package (9 ounces) frozen
  cut green beans
½ teaspoon seasoned salt
1 to 2 tablespoons butter
  or margarine

Heat oven to 350°. Place frozen green beans in ungreased 1-quart casserole. Sprinkle with salt; dot with butter. Cover and bake 30 minutes. Stir beans with fork to break apart and bake 15 minutes longer.

4 servings.

GERMAN CHOCOLATE BROWNIES

1 package (18.5 ounces)
  German chocolate cake mix
1 egg
⅓ cup water
¼ cup salad oil
1 package (9.9 ounces)
  coconut-pecan frosting mix

Heat oven to 350°. Grease baking pan, 13×9×2 inches. Mix cake mix, egg, water and oil with spoon until smooth. Spread in pan. Bake 30 to 35 minutes. Cool. Prepare frosting mix as directed on package; frost brownies. Cut into 2-inch squares.

2 dozen brownies.

Acorn squash, with its dark-green corrugated shell, has a gay scallop-edged look when you cut it in half crosswise. A little paring on the ends will serve to keep the halves from tipping when you bake them. Or cut the squash in half lengthwise; the grooves will help to steady the halves naturally. Then if you'd like to add a special (but easy) festive touch to this menu, use the baked squash halves as individual serving cups for the green beans. Dot with bits of bright pimiento for a colorful garnish.

ALL-AMERICAN SPECIAL

Pork and Peppers
Baked Chili Corn on the Cob
Shredded Lettuce Salad
Peanut Bread
with Whipped Honey Butter
Rum Baked Pineapple

Pictured on the cover

OVEN SCHEDULE

2 hours 45 minutes before serving:
   Bake pork (place on lower rack of oven).
1 hour 55 minutes before serving:
   Bake bread (place on lower rack of oven).
1 hour before serving:
   Bake corn (place on upper rack of oven).
15 minutes before serving:
   Add vegetables to pork.
5 minutes before serving:
   Increase oven temperature to 425°.
   Bake pineapple (place on lower rack of oven).
If using a larger oven (30-inch), all foods can be baked on one rack.

PORK AND PEPPERS

¼ pound Italian link sausages
   or pork link sausages, cut
   into ½-inch pieces
2 cloves garlic, finely chopped
2 tablespoons salad oil
3½- to 4-pound pork shoulder
1 medium onion, chopped
1 cup boiling water
1 chicken bouillon cube
½ teaspoon salt
¼ teaspoon pepper
2 large tomatoes, peeled and
   chopped
3 green peppers, cut into rings
1 onion, sliced and separated
   into rings
Gravy (right)

In Dutch oven or deep skillet, cook and stir sausage and garlic in oil until meat is brown; remove meat and garlic from pan. Brown roast in Dutch oven. Drain off fat. Add sausage mixture, chopped onion, water, bouillon cube, salt and pepper to Dutch oven. Cover and bake in 325° oven until roast is tender, about 2½ hours. Add tomatoes, green pepper and onion rings; bake 10 minutes.

Remove meat and vegetables to warm platter; keep warm. Make Gravy; serve with meat.

4 servings.

GRAVY

Meat broth
¼ cup cold water
2 tablespoons flour
Salt and pepper

Skim fat from meat broth. Measure broth; if necessary, add enough water to measure 1 cup and pour into Dutch oven. Shake ¼ cup water and the flour in tightly covered jar until smooth. Stir into broth. Heat to boiling, stirring constantly. Boil and stir 1 minute. Season with salt and pepper.

About 1¼ cups.

BAKED CHILI
CORN ON THE COB

¼ cup soft butter or margarine
¼ teaspoon salt
½ teaspoon chili powder
4 ears frozen corn

Heat oven to 325°. Mix butter, salt and chili powder; spread generously on each ear frozen corn. Wrap each ear in heavy-duty aluminum foil. Place on ungreased baking sheet. Bake until tender, about 1 hour.

4 servings.

VARIATION
Herbed Corn on the Cob: Substitute basil leaves, crushed rosemary leaves, marjoram or celery seed for the chili powder.

NOTE: A plastic cooking bag, about 10×15 inches, can be substituted for the aluminum foil. Place ears of corn in bag and secure end of bag with twist tie. Place in baking dish and punch 6 holes in top of bag. Bake until tender, about 1 hour.

Most versatile of lettuce varieties is iceberg, an especially good performer if a recipe calls for shredding, cutting into wedges or forming lettuce cups. Get your money's worth by choosing a compact head that feels heavy for its size. It should give slightly when you squeeze it. To shred lettuce, first cut the head in half lengthwise and place it flat side down on a cutting board. Slice down with a thin-bladed knife, trying for skinny strips. Liven up the color with sliced radishes, shredded carrots or diced celery if you like, then dress with oil and vinegar.

PEANUT BREAD WITH WHIPPED HONEY BUTTER

1 package active dry yeast
1 cup warm water (105 to 115°)
2 tablespoons sugar
4 cups buttermilk baking mix
1 can (6½ ounces) cocktail
   peanuts, chopped (1⅓ cups)
Shortening

In large mixer bowl, dissolve yeast in warm water. Add sugar and 2 cups of the baking mix. Beat on medium speed 3 minutes, scraping bowl frequently, or beat 400 strokes by hand. Stir in remaining baking mix and the peanuts. Scrape batter from side of bowl. Cover and let rise in warm place until double, about 30 minutes.

Stir down batter by beating 25 strokes. Spread evenly in greased loaf pan, 9×5×3 inches. Smooth top of loaf with floured hand. Cover and let rise until double, about 35 minutes.

Heat oven to 325°. Bake until brown, about 55 minutes. Remove from pan; brush top of loaf with shortening and cool on wire rack about 1 hour. Serve slightly warm.

1 loaf.

WHIPPED HONEY BUTTER

Beat ¼ cup honey, ¼ cup soft butter and ½ teaspoon grated orange peel until fluffy.

½ cup.

RUM BAKED PINEAPPLE

1 medium pineapple
1 large orange, pared,
   sectioned and cut up
¼ cup brown sugar (packed)
2 tablespoons butter or
   margarine, softened
2 tablespoons rum

Heat oven to 425°. Do not remove top (leaves) from pineapple; cut thick slice from side of pineapple and set aside. Cut around edge of pineapple with curved knife, being careful not to cut through shell, and remove fruit from shell. Cut fruit into bite-size pieces, discarding center core.

Mix pineapple pieces, orange pieces, brown sugar, butter and rum. Pour into shell; replace pineapple slice. Wrap pineapple leaves in heavy-duty aluminum foil. Place pineapple on ungreased baking sheet. Bake until hot, about 40 minutes. Serve hot.

4 servings.

NOTE: Pineapple leaves will darken in baking. To avoid this, cut off pineapple top and set aside. After baking, attach to pineapple shell with wooden picks.

Menus pictured on the following pages: Pork Chops and Sauerkraut (pages 40-41), Spiced Spareribs and Apples (pages 46-47), Mexican Chicken and Rice (pages 60-61), Glazed Turkey Roast (pages 68-69)

MEDITERRANEAN MELANGE

Mint-glazed Roast Lamb
Bulgar Pilaf
Herbed Vegetable Bake
Fresh Spinach Salad
Apricot Pastry Puff

OVEN SCHEDULE

4 hours before serving:
Bake lamb (place on lower rack of oven)—time is approximate and may be less, depending on weight of roast.

1 hour before serving:
Bake vegetables (place on upper rack of oven).

30 minutes before serving:
Bake pilaf (place on upper rack of oven).

15 minutes before serving:
Add zucchini to vegetables.

30 minutes before serving dessert:
Increase oven temperature to 450°.
Bake dessert (place on lower rack of oven).

If using a larger oven (30-inch), all foods can be baked on one rack.

MINT-GLAZED ROAST LAMB   Select roast from those listed in timetable on page 58. Allow about ½ pound per person. Place meat fat side up on rack in shallow roasting pan. Insert meat thermometer so tip is in thickest part of meat and does not rest in fat. Roast uncovered in 325° oven until desired doneness (see timetable), using thermometer reading as final guide. During last hour of roasting, brush meat 2 or 3 times with Minted Glaze (page 56). Serve any remaining glaze as a sauce.

Roast lamb is easier to carve if allowed to set for 15 to 20 minutes after removing from oven. Since meat continues to cook after removal from oven, if roast is to set, it should be removed from oven when thermometer registers 5 to 10° lower than the desired temperature.

MINTED GLAZE

Heat 1 jar (10 ounces) mint-flavored apple jelly, 2 cloves garlic, crushed, and 1 tablespoon water, stirring constantly, until jelly is melted.

About 1¼ cups.

Timetable

Cut	Approximate Weight	Meat Thermometer Reading	Approximate Cooking Time (minutes per lb.)	Total Cooking Time
Shoulder				
Bone In	4 to 6 pounds	175 to 180°	30 to 35	2 hours to 3 hours 30 minutes
Rolled	3 to 5 pounds	175 to 180°	40 to 45	2 hours to 3 hours 45 minutes
Cushion	3 to 5 pounds	175 to 180°	30 to 35	1 hour 30 minutes to 2 hours 55 minutes
Leg	5 to 6 pounds	175 to 180°	30 to 35	2 hours 30 minutes to 3 hours 30 minutes
Boneless Leg	3 to 5 pounds	175 to 180°	35 to 40	1 hour 45 minutes to 3 hours 20 minutes

BULGAR PILAF

1 cup bulgar wheat
2 teaspoons instant chicken bouillon
1 teaspoon instant minced onion
½ teaspoon salt
2 tablespoons butter or margarine
2 cups boiling water

Heat oven to 325°. Mix all ingredients in ungreased 1-quart casserole. Cover tightly and bake until liquid is absorbed and wheat is tender, 30 minutes.

4 to 6 servings.

HERBED VEGETABLE BAKE

6 **medium carrots, cut lengthwise into quarters**
6 **small onions**
½ **teaspoon salt**
¼ **teaspoon dill weed**
¼ **teaspoon rosemary leaves**
½ **cup hot water**
4 **small zucchini, cut lengthwise into quarters**
½ **teaspoon salt**

Heat oven to 325°. In ungreased 2-quart casserole, combine carrots, onions, ½ teaspoon salt, the dill weed, rosemary leaves and hot water. Cover and bake 45 minutes. Place zucchini on top of vegetables; sprinkle with ½ teaspoon salt. Bake until vegetables are tender, about 15 minutes.

4 to 6 servings.

APRICOT PASTRY PUFF

1 **package (10 ounces) frozen puff patty shells**
⅔ **cup apricot pie filling**

Arrange frozen patty shells close together in 2 rows on ungreased jelly roll pan, 15½×10½×1 inch. Let stand *just* until thawed, 15 to 20 minutes.

Heat oven to 450°. Overlap center edges of patty shells; roll shells into rectangle, 10×8 inches. Spread pie filling lengthwise on center third of rectangle. Make 2½-inch cuts at ½-inch intervals on long sides of rectangle. Crisscross strips over filling; seal each end of pastry. Bake until golden brown, about 20 minutes. Serve warm.

4 to 6 servings.

NOTE: The filled pastry may be placed in the freezer for up to 1 hour before baking.

SOUTHERN HERITAGE

Oven-fried Chicken
Cheese-topped Potatoes
Corn-Tomato Casserole
Assorted Vegetable Relishes
Strawberry Shortcake Whirls

OVEN SCHEDULE

1 hour before serving:
Bake chicken and potatoes (place on lower rack of oven).
30 minutes before serving:
Bake vegetable casserole (place on upper rack of oven).
Turn chicken.
10 minutes before serving:
Bake shortcake (place on upper rack of oven).
If using a larger oven (30-inch), all foods can be baked on one rack.

OVEN-FRIED CHICKEN

¼ **cup shortening (part butter)**
½ **cup all-purpose flour***
1½ **teaspoons salt**
1 **teaspoon paprika**
¼ **teaspoon pepper**
3 **pounds chicken parts (legs, thighs, breasts) or one 3-pound broiler-fryer chicken, cut up**

Heat oven to 425°. In oven, melt shortening in baking pan, 13×9×2 inches. Measure flour, salt, paprika and pepper into paper or plastic bag. Shake 2 or 3 chicken pieces at a time in bag until thoroughly coated. Place skin side down in shortening. Bake uncovered 30 minutes. Turn chicken and bake until tender, 20 to 30 minutes longer.

6 servings.

*If using self-rising flour, omit salt.

CHEESE-TOPPED POTATOES

Heat oven to 425°. Scrub 6 medium baking potatoes, and if softer skins are desired, rub with shortening. Prick with fork to allow steam to escape. Bake until soft, about 1 hour.

To serve, cut crisscross gash in each top; squeeze gently until some potato pops up through opening. Season with salt and pepper. Top each with 2 tablespoons dairy sour cream and sprinkle with grated Parmesan cheese.

6 servings.

CORN-TOMATO CASSEROLE

1 can (16 ounces) whole kernel
 corn, drained
1 can (16 ounces) stewed
 tomatoes
¼ teaspoon basil or oregano
 leaves
Dash pepper
2 tablespoons dry bread
 crumbs
1 tablespoon butter or
 margarine

Heat oven to 425°. Mix corn, tomatoes, basil leaves and pepper in ungreased 1½-quart casserole. Sprinkle with bread crumbs and dot with butter. Bake uncovered until hot and bubbly, about 25 minutes. Serve in individual dishes.

6 servings.

STRAWBERRY SHORTCAKE WHIRLS

1 quart fresh strawberries or 1
 package (16 ounces) frozen
 strawberries
½ to ¾ cup sugar (if fresh
 strawberries are used)
2 cups buttermilk baking mix
3 tablespoons sugar
3 tablespoons butter or
 margarine, melted
⅓ cup milk
2 tablespoons soft butter or
 margarine
2 tablespoons sugar
2 tablespoons chopped pecans
1 teaspoon cinnamon
Vanilla ice cream or sweetened
 whipped cream

Slice fresh strawberries; sprinkle ½ to ¾ cup sugar on berries and let stand about 1 hour. If using frozen strawberries, thaw.

Heat oven to 425°. Mix baking mix, 3 tablespoons sugar, 3 tablespoons butter and the milk to form a soft dough. Knead 8 to 10 times on lightly floured cloth-covered board. Roll into rectangle, 12×6 inches, and spread with 2 tablespoons butter. Mix 2 tablespoons sugar, the pecans and cinnamon; sprinkle on rectangle. Beginning at wide edge, roll up. Seal well by pinching edge of dough into roll. Cut roll into 6 slices. Flatten each to about 2½ inches in diameter and place on ungreased baking sheet. Bake until golden brown, about 10 minutes. Serve warm, topped with ice cream and strawberries.

6 servings.

FIESTA FAVORITE

Mexican Chicken and Rice
Spinach-Cucumber Salad
Cheese Sticks
Mocha Brownie Cupcakes

Pictured on page 53

OVEN SCHEDULE

1 hour 10 minutes before serving:
    Bake chicken casserole (place on lower rack of oven).
40 minutes before serving:
    Bake cupcakes (place on upper rack of oven).
    Add rice, corn and kidney beans to chicken casserole.
15 minutes before serving:
    Bake cheese sticks (place on lower rack of oven).
If using a larger oven (30-inch), all foods can be baked on one rack.

MEXICAN CHICKEN AND RICE

3 tablespoons salad oil
**2½ to 3 pounds chicken parts
(thighs, legs, breasts) or 2½-
to 3-pound broiler-fryer
chicken, cut up**
½ cup all-purpose flour
**1 can (28 ounces) whole
tomatoes**
**1 medium onion, chopped
(about ½ cup)**
1½ teaspoons salt
1½ to 2 teaspoons chili powder
**⅛ teaspoon instant minced
garlic**
⅛ teaspoon pepper
Dash cayenne red pepper
2 chicken bouillon cubes
2½ cups boiling water
1 cup uncooked regular rice
**1 can (8 ounces) whole kernel
corn**
1 can (8 ounces) kidney beans

Heat oil in Dutch oven or large skillet; coat chicken with flour and brown over medium heat, 15 to 20 minutes. Drain off fat.

Heat oven to 350°. Mix tomatoes (with liquid) and remaining ingredients except rice, corn and beans; pour onto chicken. Cover and bake 30 minutes. Stir in rice, corn (with liquid) and beans (with liquid); bake until chicken and rice are tender and vegetables are hot, 30 to 40 minutes.

4 to 6 servings.

CHEESE STICKS

1 loaf (1 pound) French bread
¼ cup butter or margarine,
   melted
2 tablespoons grated
   Parmesan cheese

Heat oven to 350°. Cut two 4-inch pieces from bread, then cut each piece lengthwise into 6 sticks. (Use remaining bread for another meal.) Brush sticks on cut sides with butter; arrange on ungreased baking sheet. Sprinkle with Parmesan cheese. Bake until golden, about 15 minutes.

1 dozen sticks.

MOCHA BROWNIE CUPCAKES

2 eggs
¼ cup water
3 to 4 teaspoons powdered
   instant coffee
1 package (15.5 ounces) fudge
   brownie mix
½ cup chopped nuts (optional)

Heat oven to 350°. Place paper baking cups in 12 medium muffin cups. Mix eggs, water, instant coffee and brownie mix with spoon until smooth. Stir in nuts. Spoon into muffin cups, filling each ⅔ full. Bake 25 to 30 minutes. Tops will be shiny, cracked and slightly soft to the touch. Serve with cinnamon or vanilla ice cream if you like.

1 dozen cupcakes.

When the attraction in the center ring is "hot," keep the accompanying acts "cool." Loosely, that's the rule of thumb applied here. The Mexican main dish is typically spicy, so the salad, a combination of raw spinach and thin-sliced cucumber, is gently flavored. Be sure to wash spinach well, removing stems and damaged leaves. Toss with a mild herb dressing. Chopped salted peanuts would be a fine garnish.

GATEWAY TO THE EAST

Chicken Oriental
Parsleyed Rice
Chinese Pea Pods
Pickled Vegetables (cauliflower, carrots, cucumbers)
Mandarin Plums
Tea

OVEN SCHEDULE

1 hour 15 minutes before serving:
Bake chicken (place on lower rack of oven).
30 minutes before serving:
Bake rice (place on lower rack of oven) and plums (place on upper rack of oven).
If using a larger oven (30-inch), all foods can be baked on one rack.

CHICKEN ORIENTAL

Salad oil
3 to 4 pounds chicken parts (legs, thighs, breasts)
1 jar (3 ounces) sliced mushrooms
1 can (10½ ounces) condensed cream of chicken soup or cream of mushroom soup
¾ cup sauterne or dry sherry*
1 teaspoon salt
½ teaspoon thyme leaves
¼ cup diced green pepper
¼ cup chopped onion
1 can (5 ounces) water chestnuts, drained and sliced

Heat ⅛ inch oil in large skillet; brown chicken over medium heat, 15 to 20 minutes. Place chicken in ungreased 2½-quart casserole or baking pan, 13×9×2 inches. Mix mushrooms (with liquid) and remaining ingredients; pour onto chicken. Cover and bake in 350° oven until chicken is tender, 1 to 1¼ hours.

4 to 6 servings.

*You can substitute ¾ cup apple juice and 3 tablespoons sherry flavoring for the sauterne or dry sherry.

PARSLEYED RICE

2 cups boiling water or chicken broth
1 cup uncooked regular rice
1 teaspoon salt
2 tablespoons snipped parsley

Heat oven to 350°. Mix all ingredients except parsley in ungreased 1- or 1½-quart casserole. Cover tightly and bake until liquid is absorbed and rice is tender, about 30 minutes. Stir in parsley.

4 to 6 servings.

MANDARIN PLUMS

2 cans (16 ounces each) purple plums, drained (reserve syrup)

1 can (11 ounces) mandarin orange segments, drained

¼ cup sugar

½ teaspoon cinnamon

¼ teaspoon ginger

Heat oven to 350°. Combine plums and orange segments in ungreased 1½-quart casserole. Mix reserved plum syrup, the sugar, cinnamon and ginger; pour onto fruits. Cover and bake until hot, about 30 minutes. Serve warm.

4 to 6 servings.

If you find fresh Chinese pea pods (sometimes called snow peas) in your supermarket or specialty store, snip off the tips, "string" as you would fresh green beans, and cook very briefly so they stay crisp. Even quicker are frozen pea pods; follow the package directions.

Pickled vegetables are easy to come by on your supermarket shelf, bottled either individually or as a pickled mix. Not that it's any great chore to fix your own: Slice up an onion and a couple of carrots and cut about 4 celery stalks into short strips. Make a simple one-to-one pickling mixture: 1 cup vinegar, 1 cup water, 1 cup sugar, 1 tablespoon salt. Heat to boiling, stirring occasionally. Pour this hot syrup over the vegetables in a jar or bowl. Cover and refrigerate at least 4 hours.

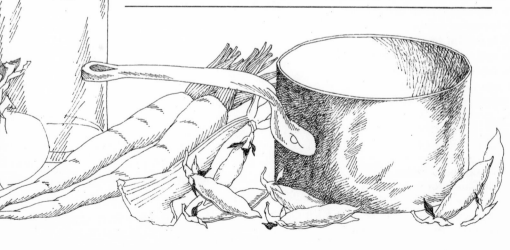

FAMILY FLAIR

Chicken and Dressing Casserole
Green Bean-Tomato Medley
Molded Gelatin Salad
Ginger-Applesauce Squares

OVEN SCHEDULE

1 hour 15 minutes before serving:
Bake chicken casserole (place on lower rack of oven).
40 minutes before serving:
Bake dessert (place on upper rack of oven).
20 minutes before serving:
Bake vegetables (place on lower rack of oven).
If using a larger oven (30-inch), all foods can be baked on one rack.

CHICKEN AND DRESSING CASSEROLE

¼ cup salad oil
½ cup all-purpose flour
1 teaspoon salt
½ teaspoon paprika
¼ teaspoon pepper
2½- to 3-pound broiler-fryer chicken, cut up
1 can (10½ ounces) condensed cream of chicken soup or cream of mushroom soup
6 cups soft bread cubes
1 medium onion, chopped (about ½ cup)
¾ cup chopped celery
¼ cup butter or margarine, melted
1 cup milk
1 teaspoon salt
½ teaspoon sage
½ teaspoon thyme leaves
¼ teaspoon pepper

Heat oil in large skillet. Mix flour, 1 teaspoon salt, the paprika and ¼ teaspoon pepper; coat chicken. Brown chicken in oil over medium heat 15 to 20 minutes. Place in ungreased 2½-quart casserole or baking dish, 13½×9×2 inches. Pour soup onto chicken.

Heat oven to 350°. Measure remaining ingredients into large bowl and toss. Mound mixture on chicken. Cover and bake until chicken is tender, 1 to 1¼ hours.

4 to 6 servings.

GREEN BEAN-TOMATO MEDLEY

2 cans (16 ounces each) Italian
    green beans, drained
1 can (4 ounces) button
    mushrooms, drained
2 tomatoes, cut into 1-inch
    wedges
1 teaspoon salt
⅛ teaspoon pepper
2 tablespoons butter or
    margarine

Heat oven to 350°. Combine beans and mushrooms in ungreased 1½-quart casserole; top with tomato wedges. Sprinkle with salt and pepper and dot with butter. Cover and bake until hot, about 20 minutes.

4 to 6 servings.

GINGER-APPLESAUCE SQUARES

1 package (14.5 ounces)
    gingerbread mix
1 cup applesauce
½ cup raisins
½ cup finely chopped nuts
Whipped cream, ice cream or
    applesauce

Heat oven to 350°. Grease and flour baking pan, 9×9×2 inches. Prepare gingerbread mix as directed on package except—decrease water to ¼ cup and add applesauce. Stir in raisins and nuts. Spread in pan. Bake 35 to 40 minutes. Cool slightly. Cut 4 to 6 servings from cake. Serve warm, topped with whipped cream. Use remaining cake for another meal.

4 to 6 servings.

VARIATION
Ginger-Applesauce Bars: Pour batter into greased and floured jelly roll pan, 15½×10½×1 inch. Bake 12 to 15 minutes. Cool. Dust with confectioners' sugar and cut into bars, 3½×1 inch. Serve with ice cream or applesauce.

3 dozen bars.

HEN PARTY

Herbed Cornish Hens
Stuffed Potato Salad
Lemon-baked Asparagus
Orange-Onion-Avocado Salad
Chocolate Parfaits

OVEN SCHEDULE

1 hour 15 minutes before serving:
   Bake potatoes (place on lower rack of oven).
1 hour before serving:
   Bake Cornish hens (place on lower rack of oven).
20 minutes before serving:
   Bake asparagus (place on upper rack of oven).
10 minutes before serving:
   Bake stuffed potatoes.
If using a larger oven (30-inch), all foods can be baked on one rack.

HERBED CORNISH HENS

4 Rock Cornish hens (about 1 pound each)
Salt and pepper
½ cup butter or margarine, melted
½ teaspoon thyme leaves
½ teaspoon marjoram leaves

Thaw hens if frozen. Heat oven to 400°. Rub cavities of hens with salt and pepper. Place hens breast side up on rack in shallow roasting pan. Mix butter, thyme leaves and marjoram leaves; brush hens with part of butter mixture. Roast until tender and golden brown, 50 to 60 minutes, brushing hens occasionally with remaining butter mixture during baking period.

4 servings.

The Rock Cornish hen could easily have qualified as the original "Chicken Little," as it's the smallest member of the chicken family. Even though it weighs only 1 to 1½ pounds, it's very meaty for its size; one of the bigger hens will usually serve two. The place to find them, year round, is the freezer section of the supermarket. To vary the flavor of the hens, try substituting 2 tablespoons lemon juice, 1 teaspoon tarragon leaves and 1 teaspoon snipped chives for the thyme and marjoram leaves in the recipe. Or try these versatile little fellows stuffed and roasted, or split and broiled or fried.

STUFFED POTATO SALAD

4 medium baking potatoes
¼ to ⅓ cup milk
1 cup shredded lettuce
3 tablespoons dairy sour cream, mayonnaise or salad dressing
½ teaspoon lemon juice
¼ teaspoon onion powder
¼ teaspoon salt
½ cup shredded Cheddar cheese

Heat oven to 400°. Scrub potatoes, and if desired, rub with shortening for softer skins. Prick with fork to allow steam to escape. Bake until tender, about 1 hour.

Cut thin slice from top of each potato; scoop out insides, leaving thin shells. Mash potato until no lumps remain; add milk in small amounts, beating after each addition. Stir in lettuce, sour cream, lemon juice, onion powder, salt and ¼ cup of the cheese. Fill potato shells with mashed potato mixture and sprinkle with remaining cheese. Bake until potatoes are hot and cheese is melted, about 10 minutes.

4 servings.

LEMON-BAKED ASPARAGUS

1 to 1¼ pounds fresh asparagus or 1 package (10 ounces) frozen asparagus spears
¼ cup butter or margarine, melted
1 teaspoon lemon juice
½ teaspoon salt

Heat oven to 400°. Break off tough ends of asparagus as far down as stalks snap easily; wash spears and drain. (If using frozen asparagus, rinse with small amount of running cold water to separate and remove ice crystals; drain.) Arrange asparagus in single layer in ungreased baking dish, 11¾×7½×1½ inches. Cover tightly with aluminum foil and bake until tender, about 20 minutes (for frozen, about 30 minutes). Mix butter, lemon juice and salt; drizzle on asparagus.

4 servings.

GOOD GOBBLER

Glazed Turkey Roast
Broccoli and Stuffing Casserole
Baked Tomatoes
with Dill Sauce
Mixed Green Salad
Lemon Sherbet Pie

Pictured on page 54

OVEN SCHEDULE

3 hours 20 minutes before serving:
  Bake turkey roast (place on lower rack of oven)—time is approximate and may be less, depending on weight of roast and directions on package.

1 hour 10 minutes before serving:
  Reduce oven temperature to 350° if necessary. Bake pie shell (place on upper rack of oven).

50 minutes before serving:
  Bake broccoli casserole (place on lower rack of oven).

20 minutes before serving:
  Bake tomatoes (place on upper rack of oven).

If using a larger oven (30-inch), all foods can be baked on one rack.

GLAZED TURKEY ROAST

3- to 4-pound frozen boneless turkey roast (without gravy)
Glaze (below)

Roast frozen turkey roast as directed on package except—50 minutes before roast is done, reduce oven temperature to 350° if necessary. Continue roasting until done, brushing with Glaze 2 or 3 times during roasting period. Let roast stand at room temperature 20 minutes for easier slicing.

6 servings.

NOTE: If package directions are not available, heat oven to 350°. Rub lightly with salt and pepper if roast is not pre-seasoned. Place on rack in shallow baking pan and brush with melted butter. Roast until done, 2½ to 3 hours, inserting meat thermometer in center after 2 hours. About 50 minutes before roast is done, brush with Glaze. Continue roasting until meat thermometer registers 170 to 175°, brushing with remaining glaze 1 or 2 times during baking period.

GLAZE

Mix ⅓ cup orange or lemon marmalade, 3 tablespoons chili sauce and ½ teaspoon dry mustard.

BROCCOLI AND STUFFING CASSEROLE

2 cups milk
1 cup shredded process
   American cheese (about 4
   ounces)
1 teaspoon marjoram leaves
1 teaspoon celery salt
1 teaspoon crushed sage leaves
½ teaspoon salt
4 eggs
3 cups plain croutons
1 package (10 ounces) frozen
   chopped broccoli, thawed

Heat oven to 350°. Heat milk, cheese, marjoram leaves, celery salt, sage leaves and salt in 2-quart saucepan, stirring constantly, until cheese is melted and mixture is smooth. Beat eggs until blended; stir hot mixture slowly into eggs. Stir in croutons and broccoli. Pour into greased 1½-quart casserole. Bake until center is set, 40 to 50 minutes.

6 servings.

NOTE: Use commercially prepared croutons. Or trim crusts from 4 slices buttered bread. Cut bread into ⅜-inch cubes. Spread on an ungreased baking sheet; bake in 350° oven until golden brown, about 15 minutes.

BAKED TOMATOES WITH DILL SAUCE

⅓ cup dairy sour cream
3 tablespoons mayonnaise or
   salad dressing
1 to 2 tablespoons finely
   chopped onion
½ teaspoon dill weed
½ teaspoon salt
¼ teaspoon vinegar
6 medium tomatoes

Mix sour cream, mayonnaise, onion, dill weed, salt and vinegar. Cover and refrigerate until serving time.

Heat oven to 350°. Cut ½-inch slice from stem end of each tomato. Place tomatoes cut sides up in ungreased baking dish, 10×6×2 inches, or individual baking dishes. Bake uncovered until tomatoes are hot, about 20 minutes. Serve with dill sauce.

6 servings.

LEMON SHERBET PIE

1½ cups chocolate wafer
   crumbs
¼ cup butter or margarine,
   melted
2 pints lemon sherbet

Heat oven to 350°. Mix crumbs and butter. Reserve 1 to 2 tablespoons of the crumb mixture for topping; press remaining crumb mixture firmly and evenly against bottom and side of 9-inch pie pan (do not press on rim). Bake until firm, about 10 minutes. Cool 30 minutes.

Fill with sherbet; top with reserved crumb mixture. Freeze until serving time.

FISH FOR COMPLIMENTS

Fish au Gratin
Duchess Potatoes
Lemon-buttered Broccoli
Mixed Green Salad
Pears 'n Berries

OVEN SCHEDULE

30 minutes before serving:
Bake fish and broccoli (place on lower rack of oven).
15 minutes before serving:
Bake potatoes (place on upper rack of oven) and dessert (place on lower rack of oven).

FISH AU GRATIN

2 packages (12 ounces each) frozen halibut steaks
1 teaspoon salt
½ teaspoon oregano leaves
2 green onions, finely chopped
1 tablespoon dry bread crumbs
2 tablespoons grated Parmesan cheese
2 tablespoons butter or margarine, melted
1 cup sauterne or chicken broth or bouillon

Heat oven to 400°. Place frozen fish in ungreased baking dish, 13½×9×2 inches. Sprinkle with salt and oregano. Mix onions, bread crumbs, cheese and butter; spread on fish. Pour sauterne into baking dish. Bake uncovered until fish flakes easily with a fork, about 30 minutes. Garnish with parsley and tomato wedges.

4 servings.

DUCHESS POTATOES

Heat oven to 400°. Prepare instant mashed potato puffs as directed on package for 4 servings except—decrease milk to 2 tablespoons. In small mixer bowl, beat 1 egg slightly; add hot potatoes and beat on medium speed until fluffy.

Drop mixture by spoonfuls (8 to 10) onto greased baking sheet. Or place in pastry tube and form rosettes. Sprinkle with paprika. Bake until golden brown, about 15 minutes.

4 servings.

LEMON-BUTTERED BROCCOLI

2 packages (10 ounces each) frozen broccoli spears
2 tablespoons butter or margarine, melted
1 tablespoon lemon juice
½ teaspoon salt

Heat oven to 400°. Rinse broccoli with small amount of running cold water to separate and remove ice crystals; drain. Place broccoli in ungreased shallow 1½-quart casserole or baking dish, 11¾×7½×1½ inches. Cover and bake until tender, 25 to 30 minutes. Mix butter, lemon juice and salt; drizzle over broccoli.

4 servings.

PEARS 'N BERRIES

1 package (10 ounces) frozen raspberries, thawed and drained (reserve syrup)
1 tablespoon cornstarch
1 can (16 ounces) pear halves, drained

Heat oven to 400°. Mix 2 tablespoons of the reserved raspberry syrup and the cornstarch in ungreased 1-quart casserole. Stir in remaining reserved syrup and the fruits. Cover and bake until syrup is thickened and fruits are hot, about 15 minutes. Serve warm.

4 servings.

FOILED AGAIN

Chilled Tomato Juice
Fish in Foil
Shoestring Potatoes
Tossed Green Bean Salad
Quick Blueberry-Peach
Shortcake

OVEN SCHEDULE

40 minutes before serving:
Bake fish (place on lower rack of oven).
20 minutes before serving:
Bake potatoes (place on upper rack of oven).
10 minutes before serving:
Uncover fish.
Stir potatoes.
Bake shortcake (place on upper rack of oven—for smaller oven, bake after potatoes have been removed).
If using a larger oven (30-inch), all foods can be baked on one rack.

FISH IN FOIL

1½ to 2 pounds frozen halibut, sole, perch or cod fillets
2 tablespoons butter or margarine, melted
2 tablespoons lemon juice
1 teaspoon salt
¼ teaspoon pepper
Paprika
Lemon wedges

Heat oven to 450°. Cut frozen fish into 6 pieces (for easier cutting, let fish stand at room temperature 10 minutes). Divide fish between 2 pieces of heavy-duty aluminum foil, 18×12 inches. Mix butter and lemon juice; brush on fish. Sprinkle with salt and pepper. Wrap fish securely in foil; place in ungreased jelly roll pan, 15½×10½×1 inch. Bake 30 minutes.

Open foil packets of fish; sprinkle with paprika. Bake uncovered until fish flakes easily with a fork, about 10 minutes. Serve with lemon wedges; garnish with parsley or celery leaves.

6 servings.

SHOESTRING POTATOES

1 package (18 ounces) frozen shoestring potatoes
Seasoned salt

Heat oven to 450°. Place potatoes on ungreased baking sheet. Bake until brown, 15 to 20 minutes, stirring once during baking period. Sprinkle with salt.

6 servings.

QUICK BLUEBERRY-PEACH SHORTCAKE

2⅓ cups buttermilk baking mix
3 tablespoons sugar
3 tablespoons butter, melted
½ cup milk
2 tablespoons soft butter
2 tablespoons sugar
¼ teaspoon nutmeg
2 cups sweetened fresh or
   frozen (thawed) blueberries
2 cups sweetened sliced fresh
   or frozen (thawed) peaches
Whipped cream

Heat oven to 450°. Mix baking mix, 3 tablespoons sugar, 3 tablespoons butter and the milk to form a soft dough. Turn onto greased baking sheet; roll or pat into rectangle, 12×8 inches. Spread 2 tablespoons butter on rectangle and sprinkle with 2 tablespoons sugar and the nutmeg. Bake until light brown, 10 to 12 minutes.

Mix blueberries and peaches. Cut shortcake into 6 pieces and top each piece with fruits and whipped cream. Serve warm.

6 servings.

VARIATION

Strawberry-Pineapple Shortcake: Substitute 1 pint strawberries, sliced and sweetened, and 1 can (8¾ ounces) crushed pineapple (with syrup) for the blueberries and peaches.

Like most good salads, this green bean toss will taste best if fixed just before dinner, while the rest of the meal is baking. You do have to plan ahead, however, so that the vegetables are already chilled when you're ready to use them. Another beforehand move: Save out some of the large outside lettuce leaves to make lettuce cups before tearing the rest of the head into bite-size pieces.

What now? Combine the lettuce bits with a large can of cut green beans and a can of mushroom stems and pieces, both drained. If you have some chopped pimiento to add for color, so much the better. Over all goes any tangy Italian dressing. Toss and then divvy up among those lettuce cups you so forsightedly set aside.

A particularly nice thing about a salad like this: You don't have to confine yourself to green beans. Almost any combination of canned cut vegetables will do. And if you have dabs of leftover vegetables—peas, carrots, cauliflower, limas or such—in the refrigerator, by all means toss them in.

ORIENT EXPRESS

Chinese-style
Tuna Casserole
Sweet-and-Sour Carrots
Cucumber-Spinach Salad
Hot Sesame Rolls
Lemon Sherbet

OVEN SCHEDULE

45 minutes before serving:
Bake tuna casserole (place on center rack of oven).
20 minutes before serving:
Bake carrots (place on center rack of oven).
Heat rolls (place on center rack of oven).

CHINESE-STYLE TUNA CASSEROLE

1 can (16 ounces) Chinese
  vegetables, drained
1 can (10½ ounces) condensed
  cream of mushroom soup
1 can (9¼ ounces) tuna,
  drained and flaked
¾ cup ¼-inch diagonal slices
  celery
1 tablespoon soy sauce
¼ teaspoon pepper
1 can (3 ounces) chow mein
  noodles

Heat oven to 350°. Mix all ingredients except noodles in ungreased 1½-quart casserole. Sprinkle noodles on top. Bake uncovered until bubbly and noodles are golden brown, 40 to 45 minutes.

4 servings.

SWEET-AND-SOUR CARROTS

1 can (16 ounces) small whole
  carrots, drained
2 tablespoons sweet-and-sour
  dressing

Heat oven to 350°. Place carrots in ungreased 1-quart casserole; drizzle with dressing. Cover and bake until carrots are hot, about 20 minutes.

4 servings.

HOT SESAME ROLLS

Wrap 4 to 6 sesame rolls in aluminum foil. Heat in 350° oven 20 minutes.

4 to 6 rolls.

INDEX